Dance Masters

Dance Masters

INTERVIEWS WITH LEGENDS OF DANCE

Janet Lynn Roseman

Routledge
New York London

Published in 2001 by
Routledge
29 West 35th Street
New York, NY 10001

Published in Great Britain by
Routledge
11 New Fetter Lane
London EC4P 4EE

10 9 8 7 6 5 4 3 2

Library of Congress Cataloging-in-Publication Data
Roseman, Janet Lynn.
    Dance masters : interviews with legends of dance / Janet Lynn Roseman.
      p. cm.
    ISBN 0-415-92951-2 — ISBN 0-415-92952-0 (pbk.)
    1.Dancers—United States—Interviews. 2. Choreographers—United States—Interviews.
    I. Title.
GV1785.AI R67 2001
792.8'028'0922—de21
[B]

                                                                00-045733

"Dance ye all.
The whole on high hath part in our dancing.
Who dances not, knows not what comes to pass."

—Jesus Christ
The Acts of John, New Testament Apocrypha, Verse 95

Contents

Preface

I have always been drawn to the dance. Movement provides me with the freedom to disengage from intellectual thought and to feel most alive. My spirit is always lifted when I surround myself with dance, whether I am discussing the art form, watching a performance, or taking a dance class—I have the same sensation of elation and excitement. Working as a dance critic has afforded me the privilege and joy to attend performances by the most exquisite dance companies in the world. There are unique moments in one's life when one's vision is expanded and one's consciousness is filled with insight, intuition, and a feeling that all is right with the world. During those rare moments, one is able to see beyond the usual. When I watch dance, I feel that I am experiencing such a heightened moment. Sitting in front of my computer after a performance, deciphering notes written in the dark, I have the chance to put everything I love onto a blank sheet of paper, paying attention to the visual and visceral images that delight or haunt me hours after a show.

I wanted to know more about the dance performances that I was watching and to explore the inner terrain of the artists who make and perform dance. What does it feel like to be lost inside of the dance? Perhaps by speaking with them I would be able to understand more deeply the power of dance as it was originally divined, as ritual, as worship, as true art—not an artificial exhibition of bodies moving into space.

I value artists who seem to be able to both embody and express elements of soul in their works. After an inspiring interview with Edward Villella, the artistic director for the Miami City Ballet, I decided to interview dance legends about their careers and philosophies, and also about subjects that are not usually articulated in dance, such as the creative process and the spiritual aspects of dance. I wanted to break the silence and taboo among many dancers about discussing these subjects, and this book attempts to demystify some of the mysteries of dancemaking and performance.

In these pages, Danny Grossman explains what it was like to "live in the work" when he danced with the Paul Taylor Dance Company and speaks at length about his sometimes painful psychological explorations while making dances. Merce Cunningham muses about his unorthodox "chance" methods; Edward Villella reflects on his stellar career; Mark Morris offers his insights about dance and music; Michael Smuin discusses his relationship with Jerome Robbins; Catherine Turocy speaks about the veiled spirits that help her choreograph; and Alonzo King talks about the influence of Spirit on his works.

These conversations have been both a gift and a revelation. Spending time with these artists has not only been a joyful and educational experience; it has been a highlight of my career. It is my wish that this book will inspire, instruct, and engage all of those who love dance as much as I do. Most of all I hope that this book will contribute to the elevation of dance arts in the twenty-first century.

I believe that these dance legends are artistic shamans offering to us the highest elements of that art form. I am grateful for their generous spirits, their gifts of time and attention, and the kindness that each of them showed to me. They trusted me with their words, and I hope that they feel that this book serves them well. And I regret that this book does not contain more women's voices.

Janet Lynn Roseman

Acknowledgments

This book was a labor of love for me. It is my wish that this book will inspire and elevate the art form of dance as much as dance has inspired and elevated me in my own life. I am deeply grateful to all of the artists in this book who so generously gave me not only their time, but their focused attention, a gift that I will forever cherish. And a special note of gratitude to Edward Villella, an artist and gentleman of the highest order, for inspiring me to create this book.

I have many people to thank. They include my parents, who offered me their home by the sea to write this book in quiet and beauty and who have always believed in my vision. I was thrilled that I was able to share with my brother, Mark, my intoxication of the dance during our research and photographic outings. My colleague and friend, Cynthia Pepper, offered keen insights about the manuscript and lovingly shared her suggestions.

I wish to extend a heartfelt "thank you" to Suzanna Tamminen for all of her efforts. Gayatri Patnaik, Matthew Byrnie, and Amy Reading at Routledge have been superior examples of cooperation and synergy in the making of this book, and I am fortunate that the manuscript landed on their desks.

I appreciate the efforts of the following people who kindly answered questions and sent pictures and materials whenever I asked. They include Linda Ronstadt, David Vaughan, Donna Richard, Trevor Carlson, Anne Patterson, Vicki Vigorito, Norton Owen, Kyra Jablonsky, Pam Hagen, Kristen McDonnell, Jennifer Llacera, Nancy Umanoff, Lesley Berson, Jamie Beth Cohen, Eva Nichols, Lisa Belvin, Dan Levenstein, Paula Tracy-Smuin, Margarete Roeder, Amy Wilson, Ginger Clark, and Kirsten Tanaka.

I was blessed by the gifts of photographs given to me by Maxine Morris, Philip Bermingham, Michael Smuin, and Catherine Turocy. And I am pleased to have the photographs of John Van Lund, Jed

Downhill, Richard Rutledge, Chantal Regnault, Gadi Dagon, Lois Greenfield, Nancy Brooker, Otto Berk, Marty Sohl, Andrew Oxenham, Phiz Mezey, Cylla von Tiedemann, Ed Buryn, and James Armstrong. Special thanks to the San Francisco Ballet for their assistance.

I am grateful to the Kittredge Fund at Harvard University, who extended their help to me when I needed it.

Thanks to my guiding-light spirits who accompany me.

1

Edward Villella

"The moment Villella bursts into view a kind of magnetic rapport snaps on between himself and the audience. As he flashes across the stage he creates the illusion that the music isn't fast enough, the ceiling isn't high enough, the stage isn't big enough to contain the dancing demon that somehow has invaded this small, five foot seven and a half mortal. Take, for example, *Tarantella*, a nine-minute ballet that Balanchine choreographed to showcase Villella's special virtuosity. With a snaggle-toothed grin stamped on his face, with a mischievous twinkle for his delectable partner, Patricia McBride, Villella soars birdlike in the air and hangs at the apogee a beat longer than gravity permits. Leaping, spinning, dashing, bouncing, he threatens to explode with vitality, ecstasy, life."

—————**David Martin, 1969**

Edward Villella has performed in some of the finest ballets ever made, courtesy of the genius of choreographer George Balanchine, including leading roles in *Apollo, Agon, Prodigal Son, A Midsummer Night's Dream, Tarantella, Bugaku,* and *Jewels.* His rise in the world of dance is a mythic tale. He began studying ballet as a child when his mother forced him to take ballet class at the School of American Ballet with his sister. Mrs. Villella wanted to keep him off the streets of the neighborhood in Queens, New York, after the young boy was knocked unconscious playing sports with his friends. Ironically, the young athlete resisted taking classes and was more than a bit embarrassed to study, but he soon fell in love with ballet and discovered that he had a great talent for it. Jerome Robbins's *Afternoon of the Faun* was inspired by Villella's dancing when the choreographer watched the teenage dancer at the School of American Ballet's studios.

When he was at Rhodes Prep he crossed paths with fellow dancer Allegra Kent. After a few years of dance study at SAB, which fed the burning conviction that he would become a classical dancer, Villella was heartbroken when his parents forced him to quit dance to attend college. He attended the New York Maritime College, where he felt like he was in "prison," desperately harboring his dream to become a classical dancer. Although he excelled in his studies and athletic endeavors, Villella missed dancing. An integral part of the program at the college involved travel, and when he visited other countries he quickly searched for the best dance studios in the area to take classes. During his senior year, he secretively attended dance classes in New York, firmly committed to creating a life of dance for himself once he graduated college. That experience was not only necessary for him to retrain his body but was necessary in all respects: body, mind, and spirit.

After graduation in 1955, he returned to the New York City Ballet, where he had danced as a youngster and trained ferociously in an effort to regain the precious years of technical training that he had missed while in school. Working his body mercilessly and without pause, Villella called upon master teacher Stanley Williams to guide him. For any other serious dancer, those lost years would

Edward Villella in studio session. *Copyright Philip Bermingham.*

have made it virtually impossible to dance professionally. However, Villella wasn't like other dancers. He was always observing, connecting, listening, pushing, and encouraging his body to perform beyond its natural capacity. Even when he was plagued with physical pain, he was able to do the seemingly impossible on stage—soaring in the air, leaping and spinning with so much velocity that the stage could barely contain his physical energies.

During his career with the New York City Ballet, he popularized the art form and breathed new vitality and virility into the dance. In an artistic world where more often the *object d'affection* was the ballerina, Villella was a notable exception, and he was quite responsible for the elevation of the male dancer in the world of ballet. When he danced, he not only conveyed the dance, he revealed it with powerful craftsmanship and great intelligence.

Mr. Balanchine created many roles for him in many ballets, including *Tarantella*, the *Rubies* section of *Jewels, A Midsummer Night's Dream,* and, perhaps his most famous role, *The Prodigal Son.* Considered one of the leading dancers in the world, and, perhaps, the best male dancer of his time, Villella was an electrifying artist and a superb athlete who was able to command both body and stage, always striving for perfect line, elevation, control, rhythm, design, and expression. Decades after he left the stage, it is still not unusual to hear his fans recall what a stunning dancer he was.

It seemed as if Villella could take on any challenge, and it wasn't unusual for him to dance not only his own rigorous repertoire, but often perform the roles of other dancers in the company, sometimes dancing two or three roles a performance. He danced with other companies as guest artist, lectured on the art of ballet, choreographed works for television appearances on "The Bell Telephone Hour" and "The Kraft Music Hall," and created three of his own ballets: *Narkissos, Shenandoah,* and *Shostakovitch Ballet Suite.* In a riveting documentary called *Edward Villella: Man Who Dances,* audiences had the unique opportunity to view the world of dance through his eyes and experiences.

In 1975, he was severely injured while performing at the Ford White House and was unable to dance. He spent the next decade lecturing on dance and working as artistic director for several ballet companies. Currently, he is the artistic and founding director for the Miami City Ballet, and has succeeded in putting this once-fledgling ballet company on the international map. Under his deft tutelage, the company has not only reigned in Florida, but their national and international reputation has earned them a significant place in the dance world. Fiercely committed to the Balanchine repertoire, Villella continues to train dancers not only in technical virtuosity but offers them a sterling education in the Balanchine aesthetic. The former resident choreographer Jimmy Gamonet de los Heros worked closely with Villella for many years and has provided the company with elegant works that aptly complement the Balanchine programs.

When he was fifty years old, many years after departing his professional career, he returned to the stage to star in Jerome Robbins's enigmatic ballet, *Watermill*. It was a willful endeavor given that Villella's injuries from a lifetime of dance had almost crippled him. Robbins cajoled Villella into starring in the piece, and before Villella had agreed to dance, Robbins cleverly announced to the press that Villella had agreed, making it virtually impossible for him to extricate himself. His performance was a physical resurrection, considering that he was dancing with a body that was host to countless foot fractures and broken bones.

He has danced for presidents, was the first male dancer invited to dance with the Royal Danish Ballet, and earned an unprecedented twenty-two encores when dancing at the Bolshoi Theatre in Moscow. He was the producer/director for the PBS specials "Dance in America" for one-and-a-half years, and won an Emmy Award in 1975 for his television production of the ballet *Harlequin*. In 1992 he published his autobiography (with writer Larry Kaplan), *Prodigal Son: Dancing for Balanchine in a World of Pain and Magic*. The book was so successful that it was reissued in 1998.

Villella has always made dance education a priority. He is eager to share his knowledge of dancemaking and performance, and continues to be one of ballet's most articulate spokesmen. For his accomplishments as an artist he has received a 1997 National

Medal of the Arts, the 1997 Kennedy Center Honors, the thirty-eighth annual Capezio Award, the National Society of Arts and Letters Award for Lifetime Achievement (and was only the fourth dance personality to receive the gold medal), the Frances Holleman Breathitt Award for Excellence, and the 1964 *Dance Magazine* Award. He was inducted into the State of Florida Artists Hall of Fame, and holds honorary degrees from Fordham University, Skidmore College, Union College, Nazareth College, and St. Thomas University.

Now in his sixth decade, Mr. Villella wears beauty deeply etched in the crevices of his face. He has an extraordinary gift for both verbal as well as physical communication, and builds his responses in conversation as carefully as he coaches his dancers in the ballet, paying full attention to form, content, and delivery. He spoke to me with authority, remarkable precision, and imagination, demonstrating in action the creative response. His knowledge about dance reflects a man who has mastered all means of expression, a man with full play of his talents. Edward Villella aims for and reaches a supreme quality in *art,* a term I use in all its force.

I was reading about your mother, Edward, and her influence in your life. She impressed me quite a bit. Can you tell me more about her?

She really was a person who was way ahead of her time, and she was terrifically frustrated, which I think added to her drive and her ambition for her children. She was an orphan and didn't have opportunity. But I was also part of that drive and that ambition to get beyond what her initial circumstances were. She discovered and developed her knowledge about nutrition and about health, and I think she was interested in things that were not necessarily the mainstream. I don't think she was fully comfortable with the mainstream.

I think she was a person who had great curiosity and wanted to have a great deal of knowledge. She discovered Adele Davis long before her nutritional work was known. We were brought up on blackstrap molasses and wheat germ.

**Did you ever speak to your mother about your early days in train-
ing as a dancer? It seemed as if she easily recognized that medium
as a vehicle for your life early on.**

We have to look at this in historical context. In the 1940s, growing
up in Queens, in an Italian-American family, children didn't have too
much to say. The parents were the law. Those early years were not my
choice. It was only later on that I was able to exercise my own choice,
and those choices became controversial. By the time I had reached
some ability, I was made to stop dancing. That was the last thing I
wanted to do. There were complications and difficulties, and they
were resolved simply by my wanting desperately to dance and to do
as much as my parents wanted from me, which was to get a college
education. I tried to do both and, needless to say, it was complicated,
but somehow I survived it.

**You really pushed yourself, and when you were dancing, you not
only danced your own roles, but everyone else's. That toll on your
body was harsh. I was watching the documentary *Man Who Dances*,
and there is a poignant moment when you are in the dressing room
and you are rubbing your legs and you said, "Speak to me legs,
speak to me."**

Well, we speak a physical language. We have our own alphabet
and our own vocabulary, and we make it into poetic gesture. When
you work as much as we were required to work—performing eight
times a week, dancing three to four ballets a night (and I had all of
the jumping roles)—you create at least inflammation, and inflammation slows you down. That slowing down can create cramps, and
cramps can stop you, and in stopping you, your body stops speaking.
That flexibility is the ability to speak, and when you've lost it, it's a
desperate situation if you really want to dance. One will go to all kinds
of measures to make that happen.

**Do you think you had an inherent trust that your body would
continue?**

There were a number of things that were going on. First of all, I
was terrifically frustrated, and I was willful, and I willed it to happen. I

wouldn't recommend that to anyone. If I had logic and sense, I would-n't have done it that way. I lost four valuable years in my development as a dancer from age sixteen to twenty, a critical time for a dancer. I was desperate to make up that time without knowledge. I really didn't know what I was doing. It was just will, force, and tension. I abused my body, and at another juncture I had to re-address, to return to a more normal state of physicality. I had a great deal of trouble with my musculature and cramps and ailments because I was unwilling to stop, and that just compounded those injuries.

Stanley Williams was instrumental in that reeducation and the healing of your body. How wonderful that you found him, since he really preserved your ability to dance for many years and continue your career.

My great fortune was that Stanley came along and redirected my approach to training. That took years, but it really saved my dancing life. It saved a lot of my physicality. I needed a fuller in-depth investi-gation of my physical potential, but I also needed to investigate my physical calamities. I had these two processes that were going on at the same time: to develop my technique and progress as a dancer. But I also needed to bring back my muscles to a normal state to re-duce the inflammations and to get rid of the cramping.

When you speak of being "willful" in your dancing, what do you mean by that?

I was very physical and loved to move, and that was the way I spoke and also who I was. I identified very closely with "the dancer." I was much more "the dancer" than "the person." I couldn't differentiate be-tween dance and the dancer and the person; it was all the same to me. I think it is always there; it's not that you go step-by-step in a process. Maybe it creates a process, but the passion, the will, the frustration, the neurotic kind of energy that is involved in all of this was available all the time. I had a single purpose. It was to be a dancer and to regain who I used to be. It was very easy for me to be buried in that identity. It was exciting and I loved every minute of it. It wasn't a negative thing at all. I wished I had stepped back every now and again and just taken a deep breath, but that was not part and parcel of who I was.

Edward, we have spoken before about a dancer's intelligence, a visceral intelligence. Can you speak more about that?

There are all kinds of intelligence, and our intelligence is movement and how you understand that movement. That's the kind of intelligence I am referring to: how you move, and also how you direct that movement. You direct the taste and the temperament and the sensuality and the dramatic aspect of it. It is what you have absorbed instinctively, but also what you have observed as a student when you were taught, coached, and directed, and without that intelligence to comprehend and give back, it gets to be pretty dull.

Do you mean the performance is dull?

I think that a dancer who has a tremendous amount of technical ability but is not mind-driven, one who has learned by rote, one who has a natural ability to receive these messages and then pass them through to the body, without the mental process, without absorbing and developing the mental process—you get a very technical dancer, which to me is very uninteresting. I don't hire technique. I hire what interests me in terms of movement, the quality of their movement and how they physicalize that musically. Those are intangibles or talents.

Can you teach talent?

I take it that you can teach "technique to talent," but you can't teach talent to anybody. You either have talent or you don't. Or if you wish to call it an intelligence, it's a specific intelligence and talent that you have to transfer information into movement that becomes acceptable, qualitative, elegant, and entertaining. Lincoln Kirstein once said that dancers have brains in their feet. It sounds like a very disparaging remark, and it might be.

You were able to bring to your dancing another dimension to the physical body that other dancers didn't possess; I am referring to your talents as an athlete, as a boxer, baseball player, etc.

It also brought a different approach to dance: the fact that I was an athlete and the fact that I was brought up by a neoclassicist, George Balanchine, who was terrifically engaged by the energy and the vitality of this country. I think that it was terrifically helpful to me because I didn't have to pose as some Renaissance or eighteenth- or nineteenth-century prince. I could be physical. I didn't have to adhere to some outmoded or foreign set of manners. To stomp around the stage and portray a prince is different from being in an abstract ballet where you have abstracted the character down to essence and poetry. Those are very, very different approaches to character and to role and to who you are on stage.

My wonder is that I had this physical ability to move as an athlete and a new kind of classicism, with an American energy mixing all of that together, and for me to put a certain amount of sophistication on top of my natural ability was terrifically fortunate.

Mr. Balanchine didn't explain the ballets to you in detail and would often make cryptic comments. For instance, for your role in *Prodigal,* he told you, "Icons, dear." Was it frustrating for you because he didn't give you more to go on?

It was frustrating to those of us who didn't have the mind or the intelligence or the curiosity or the time or the energy to go out and research. This is supposition, but I suppose that Balanchine thought it was obvious.

Really?

You never know. I think with an abstract man like that you are left to your own devices. You are left to making opinion based on your own lack of knowledge. It's really hard to speak about him and what his rhymes and reasons were and what he thought. I really don't know. My supposition is that he either expected you to instinctively, intellectually, understand, or have some background or curiosity, or he would give you such specific direction in gesture that you didn't have to think. He would provide it all for you. Quite often, he would caution us not to act. If you stop and think of it years later, I can reflect on this. The art of acting is not to act; it's to be.

Because acting can be so artificial.

Sure. Acting is artificial, but once you understand it to the level, you can make it a conditioned reflex and just let it evolve and happen and come out of you; that's a very different circumstance. I think that

Edward Villella and the Boston Ballet in *Apollo*.
Copyright John Van Lund. Courtesy of Jacob's Pillow.

Edward Villella and the Boston Ballet in *Apollo*. *Copyright John Van Lund. Courtesy of Jacob's Pillow.*

is what he wanted; he didn't want people to interpret it without enough understanding.

When you teach his works to your company, do you use visual images at all when working on the ballets?

What I try to do when I pass on a role is not to ask the dancer to imitate what I had previously done, or for that matter to imitate what someone else has done previously. If there is a video and they have seen the performance, I will ask them to think about it and analyze it. Then I will give them a breakdown of my approach.

Can you give me an example?

For instance, for *Rubies, Apollo,* or Tchaikovsky's *Pas de Deux,* or *Tarantella,* or *Bugaku,* I will begin to construct the role, an approach to the role, and as I do that, I will pass on anything and everything that was passed on to me, those cryptic remarks by Balanchine, or other research that I have done, or what Stanley Williams told me. Whatever information I have that is pertinent to that particular role, I will pass on. Therefore, what I do is create the parameters of the role, boundaries that should not be crossed, and, within the context of those parameters, offer three or four different approaches so that a dancer is not locked into something that is unfamiliar or uncomfortable to them.

It must be challenging to pass on a role considering that the part was made especially for you. How do you select the dancers?

If you analyze it, Balanchine made these things for us so they were comfortable to our abilities. That is why it is so hard to pass these roles on without asking a dancer to imitate them. No dancer is the same, so it doesn't make sense to me. Casting is critical, and it makes sense to me to choose a dancer who has an inclination towards that particular role, the style, the musicality, the physicality, and the attack, then to allow that dancer to have as much information and understanding as possible, and to allow them to make their own comment while I continue to guide them. It's a real molding of the role without pouring it into the mold that it came from.

Mr. Balanchine's remark that "ballet is woman" is legendary, and yet he gave you extraordinary roles. Your artistry elevated the status for men in ballet. I would like you to comment on that.

Balanchine for sure was moved to exercise his gifts by the stimulation of the muses, and the muses were for him these wonderful ballerinas, the women. He loved women, he adored them, he had deep regard and deep respect for them. They inspired him. These are clichés, but clichés because they are proven. One can understand why he would have this deep regard, because these women were inspirations for him and they unlocked his abilities and talents. Not that I think that his abilities and talents were ever locked, because they seemed to overflow all the time. I think he was a great artist, a genius, but also a technician. He was a craftsman and in order to craft a work, you need all of the elements.

Ballet by its structure and form is more of a feminine focus because men present women. When a man and a woman are onstage and they are dancing together, that is one thing, and when they are dancing separately, that's another thing. But when they are dancing together, the man is servicing the woman. Again, one can more easily understand the statement that ballet is woman. First of all, they are an inspiration, and secondly, men present them, and as gentleman, we look after them onstage.

What was it like for you to present a woman onstage?

It's a wonderful masculine feeling to look after a woman onstage. There is an odd chivalry about it, an old, wonderful, intrinsic sense. There will be people who will dispute this, but I am here to tell you that for me, it was wonderful—a wonderful thing to look after a woman. It was also very instinctive and very comfortable. I loved doing it, and in it's own way, it almost suggests that the man is the secondary character. Plus the man doesn't have pointe, so we only have two levels: a flat toe and a half-toe. A woman has those two plus full pointe, so the woman is better prepared to do so much more, to be that much more important.

The ballets he made for you were so focused on male energies.

I think it was unavoidable for him to make wonderful work for men because of the music. There are passages in the music that lend themselves to pas de trois, to pas de deux, to variations, and within all of that, this variation may suggest a feminine approach or that might suggest a male approach. You have to have a man to present a woman; you need that balance visually. In my case, when he found pieces of music that suited, and because I had a pyrotechnical technique and I had speed and I could jump and beat and do tricks, he used those abilities and related them within the music. Whether he thought ballet was "woman" or not, he was true to the moment, to the purpose, to the music, to the style. Out of that we all benefited. He made some of the best roles in history for men: *Apollo* and *Prodigal Son,* two incredible roles for male dancers. It's like a *Giselle* and a *Swan Lake.*

Did he ever speak to you about the sacred elements of dance?

He was a deeply religious man. He was also a man who understood old philosophies and old approaches, and understood the celestial aspects, the astronomical, and the numerical approaches of the great artists of the past. I'm not the right person to talk to about this subject because I don't have any background or knowledge, but he might have even had this metaphysical approach to things.

Did he ever speak about those aspects with you?

He would talk about all kinds of things, but they would be so abstract. He would talk for a time and ask, "Does time pass or do we pass through time?" He would pose these fascinating statements. He might discuss it ever so briefly and move on to something else. He was a man beyond a lot of us, and certainly beyond me. I refer to myself as "nearly a mere mortal" in his presence.

During performance, did you ever sense that there was something higher, perhaps a more spiritual or elevated state that you were experiencing?

That has not been my experience. I think these things are less spiritual than practical and real. Yes, you do separate yourself from the reality of the moment, but you are controlling reality, finally. Your reality comes from another sense of reality; it becomes an abstract.

You are hiding your reality to deal with an abstract reality, rather than realistically pushing the gears to make something happen; you have automatic transmission so that all of this transpires.

I don't think there was ever a time for spiritualisms or mysticisms; it was just very practical, achieving the technique and through that technique eliminating interference and getting it down to reflex. That's craft. You hone that craft to the point where it becomes artistry. I was never mystically or religiously or spiritually moved to make a performance. It was always work, day-to-day work. Even if you make great art, it is day-to-day work.

I know that often when Mr. Balanchine was working on a ballet, he would teach it out of sequence, much like the manner in which a film director would shoot a movie. Conceptually, I would think that this would be difficult to learn that way.

It was and it wasn't, because that is the way he presented everything. There was no full conception explained to you; there was no full approach explained about the musicality, or the philosophy, or the period. He would just begin choreographing. He spoke to you mostly with his body, and you had to understand immediately what you saw. You had to have this visceral intelligence that took the picture and digested it and allowed your mind to then place it within your own body, imitating it until you got it, and sensed it, and felt it, and moved forward with it. Basically, he just wanted to work and he didn't want to talk about it.

After all the years you worked together, could you sense telepathically what he wanted you to do without speaking? Was there any type of silent but known communication between you?

Telepathically . . . one would have to say a word that would suggest one body observing and absorbing. My body as well as my eyes were helping me absorb this. That's what you do. You stand there and watch and you begin to decipher. It's like saying the line "I love you." How many ways can you say it? You can say it a thousand different ways. It's the same with gesture. That's why you have to not add, you have to eliminate. You have to get down to the essence of what it is, and it's not your intelligence, your mind, and your talent. Your eyes are absorbing from the person who is demonstrating. It's body to body and mind to mind.

The wonder of Balanchine beyond all the other stuff is that he was a fabulous dancer and he wore style. When he walked in and began to demonstrate, it was a demonstration that had all of the technical components, but it had the style, it had the period, it had the demeanor, it had the natural relationships available about how one would behave as a particular character.

You begin to have this understanding without having full knowledge and full comprehension. It would begin to arrive. One of the things that I miss most about dancing is making a role. There are a lot of people who worked who basically imitated and just did what he showed them, without trying to get underneath it and behind it and investigate. I think a lot of them missed so much because they aren't just steps to music. These are things that he thought about up to a decade before he put a step to music.

Given that chance to go so much further in the role, wouldn't that make the work so much more rewarding?

Let me put it this way: If you learn something, it takes a long time to acquire it and you think you will never get it. Now a year or so later, you got it. Now you are prepared for the next step. If you are where you are long enough, you might get a little bored with it and want to go to the next step to see what is available. Your curiosity and your sense of exploration is evolving and developing. So you go step by step.

And in that exploration you are really becoming an artist.

Yes. You go from student to dancer to performer and, hopefully, finally, the artist. That's the ultimate. I don't want to see someone's technique; I go to see someone's mind driving their technique. It's a very, very different idea. The artists are people who take that information and allow their minds to participate without stepping over the parameters, to fully develop what is available. There are such dimension to these ballets. Balanchine networked these works with many points of departure, many references, historically, philosophically, and artfully. This was a man who was fully versed.

I'd like to speak about working with Jerry Robbins, and I understand his approach was very different from working with Mr. Balanchine.

It was fascinating to work with Jerry. The first time I worked with him was in *Afternoon of a Faun*. Jerry was not only a choreographer, he was a director, and Balanchine was not that. He hardly ever spoke other than with his body, but Jerry gave you all kinds of images and points of departure, theatrically and dramatically. He gave you substantial images, so it was very, very different.

Can you identify the differences between both men?

Jerry liked to see it. He would see it, and then think of an alternative or a variation on it, then he would develop a variation without losing the material that it came from. He kept developing, and he would develop around an idea or a series of ideas, and you would have three or four different versions. You would learn those versions, and as time went by he would reduce it and take the best and begin to put it into that single, cohesive substance. It was very different work from Balanchine's, who would allow you to influence the work. It's rare that Jerry would allow you to influence the work. He had preconceived notions about exactly how it should be, whereas Balanchine was freer, and as he saw the work on you, he would adjust it for you. Jerry wanted you to adjust toward his already in-depth, complete sense of gesture.

Did Mr. Robbins give you all the different variations until he thought he had perfected It?

Absolutely. He was always searching for what it finally would be, or should be. The difference of course is that Jerry wanted to see it and Balanchine already knew it. Each had terrifically valid approaches.

Did it make you crazy to learn all of the variations? Wasn't that frustrating for you, and a lot of information to retain and change at his bidding?

It was a great deal of information to keep in your head when you have twenty or thirty ballets that are also currently in the repertoire for that season.

It's part of the intelligence that is needed or required to be a dancer. That wasn't my forte, memory.

I am surprised to hear that.

I had a real problem with memory, and I had to work very, very hard. I found that it was my body that remembered, and I had muscle memory more than intellectual memory.

I know you were in a brawl when you were younger. Are the memory problems because of that incident?

I think it was. I remember having a photographic memory, and after the beating I've struggled with memory ever since. Who knows? I have always struggled with this from my twenties on.

What helped you remember the works?

It was important to know the counts, and if you knew the counts you had another basis to refer. The other thing that helped me was to know what connected the step. In other words, all of these movements are not done in a single running line; they are done in a series of eight counts or fours or three, or there is a particular phrase. If you get the phrase and it is directly related to a choreographic phrase, how you leave that phrase and get to the next phrase might also be how you leave the last step and get to the next step. How you connect those steps was a terrific aid to my memory.

Before your performances, you said that you would clear out your mind. This "clearing out" sounds very Zen to me. What did you experience moments before you went onstage to perform?

What I preferred to do was to know a role well enough to have enough confidence in that knowledge, and to develop it to the degree that I was comfortable with it, to allow my natural instincts and my natural abilities to take over onstage. What you don't want to see is the gesture coming at you. You want to see it as though it is happening for the very first time.

My thoughts about that was to eliminate, to stop thinking about it, to get my mind absolutely clear, to clear the decks and have an empty canvas. The moment I stepped onstage, the music began, and whatever else that was brought to memory in what I was required to do would happen—not that I would make it happen, but it came from the inside of me, rather than the outside of me. I wanted it to have that kind of spontaneity, plus I didn't want to think onstage. I didn't want to calculate and drive it. You end up doing it later because you are aware. I would prefer that it was an awareness that was almost floating above the stage, observing what was going on, so as not to interfere with the actual actions that were taking place.

Did you visualize yourself performing before you went on?

I did all of that in the rehearsal process. I wasn't into all of these mystical things. I am a blue-collar kid from Queens. I just wanted to step onstage and have nothing interfere with that moment and those series of movements until I was offstage. I wanted to be completely in character without interference and make it totally and completely spontaneous. Meanwhile, a *great* deal of energy and effort was going on. It's incumbent upon us to make the difficult look easy. Dancers are a more sophisticated, theatricalized kind of athlete, so it's poetry.

Speaking of poetry, my favorite ballet is *Bugaku*. I've seen it performed by the San Francisco Ballet, but I wish I had the chance to watch you dance that ballet. It is so elegant and striking and erotic.

I think that the most important thing in *Bugaku* is not to indulge the obvious. There are erotic and sensual overtones to that work. The key was not to overindulge what was available. The premise that "the art of acting is not to act but to make it happen" was key, but it was also key in terms of who the person I was working with was. Allegra Kent was phenomenal to work with because she had an incredible distance about her and yet she was fully engaged with you. There were so many incredible elements that were exchanged between us. Her portrayal and our ability to communicate with unspoken understanding was already key to the approach to that role. But the gesture, the music, and the style also supported what it was that we were doing. The danger was to overdo because it was already there.

I remember watching Balanchine and having this inner sense and the ability to emanate from the core of who you are, not just from your spine but from the core of who you are, not only as a human being but also how you have digested and now return to us this other core. You arrive at the core of this character that you are portraying, that you have the essence of.

Didn't you have the chance to see the dancers from the Imperial Court perform when you were in Japan?

Yes. I was in Japan in 1958 or 1959. We had the opportunity to see the Imperial Court dancers who were the inspiration for this ballet. Lincoln Kirstein invited the Gagaku to perform with the New York City Ballet within one of the programs. I already had a sense of what this was and where Balanchine was going with it. Just watching his body and hearing his body as it spoke to me, I had a pretty good point of departure.

When you performed it years later after the premiere, was it a different experience for you?

In a funny way, I liked it better when I was first doing it. I think it was fresher, and I think, as time went on, the thought process didn't stop. At some point I would have loved to have resisted the thought process from going any further, because I think I had gotten to the point where I wanted it and I couldn't help but solidify it. I don't think I went too far afield, but it was probably a little more solid than what I wanted it to be.

Edward, what do you mean, solid?

A little heavy, a little more three-dimensional. I think a little more of that mystery would have helped.

I understand that Mr. Balanchine asked Hermes Pan to choreograph a piece for the company, but due to scheduling differences he was unable to do it. Were you aware of this?

This is not something I can verify, but my dim recollection of that time was that Balanchine wanted to invite Fred Astaire to perform with the company.

That's great. What year did this happen?

It was either the late 1950s or the early 1960s. I think he wanted to use the Modern Jazz Quartet and have them make a piece, and he would make a piece to that music using Fred Astaire. Balanchine had terrific regard for Fred Astaire, for his style and musicality and his elegance. He was the most immaculate musical mover I had ever seen. The only person close to him was Balanchine. He wanted to pay respect to him. They were two very elegant men. It would have been a historic program.

At rehearsal today, I was watching the men in the company rehearse, and there were three of them leaping through the air beautifully. I thought how wonderful it must feel to "fly" in the air like that. You possessed this ability to soar. Can you tell me what it felt like?

For me, it was a sense of soaring and stopping and moving on. It was wonderful because it's this idea of thrusting yourself through space with abandon, yet you have full and total control. That's a wonderful feeling to have—that sense of total freedom as if you have completely given in to whatever is there and available, and yet you are not lost in it. You still control it. It's a wonderful sensation; it's a wonderful, sensual feeling. It's a terrific sensual feeling when you feel the warmth of your body, which is unbelievably trained and rehearsed and ready and it produces your intent. It is a sensation just to feel each part of your body as it leads.

We don't dance straight on and flat. There is an undulation that is constantly going on within our bodies because we turn out. We are turning out, forward, and out, and when you move, you are extending the turn out. Every time you are moving, there is undulation that goes on, and it goes on from the feet, from the arches of the ankles, and passes straight up through the body, so your whole body is participating in a single, propulsive gesture. Your entire body is moving in a cohesive, elegant, formal way, and yet it's soft and beautiful.

Is there any type of vibratory sensation?

No, it's more of a thrust, a propulsion. You push away and you soar or you move across the floor. Even if you aren't jumping you get

Edward Villella in studio session. *Copyright Philip Bermingham.*

the same sort of sense of it. If you think in terms of movement against technique, then you always move up, forward, and out. You don't achieve a position, satisfy, and then go on. That satisfaction and position that you are achieving is part of a continuous line. That to me is dancing.

You are speaking about the fluidity of the movement?

It is the fluidity; it is the continuity. It is the connecting element of the gesture as you pass through all of these positions and steps. That continuity gives it a sense of the dance.

Do you miss dancing, Edward? You must.

I miss it desperately. It's a sensation and a feeling that is very hard to be without if you have been with it so long. When you can't do it the same way you previously did, you know you are missing the ultimate. I can approximate it a little bit when I move in class and demonstrate, but there isn't any way I can touch what it used to be. There is this wonderful memory sense. It's a body muscular memory, but it is also a memory of sensation and sensuality. I don't want to overdramatize this, but it leaves you knowing that the past will never be repeated. There is a certain finality about that part of it, and, therefore, when you have that kind of sense and passion about dance, you have to come to terms with it, and it takes time.

Would you ever consider dancing again?

No, I am not capable of dancing again. I have two artificial hips and nine broken toes and stress fractures in both legs and a bad back and inoperable knees and a bad neck. After all, we are the summation of all the abuse we provided ourselves.

Do you consider *Watermill* as your farewell, since you didn't have the chance to have an official departure from dancing?

I had no choice. My career was stopped abruptly. I was in the middle of the *Corsaire* pas de deux at the White House, and I had this incredible burning pain that was so sharp I was awake the whole night. *Watermill* was a work that was done when I was still a dancer, but the demands of the work were much more theatrical and dramatic than they were technical. It still took a tremendous amount of experience to pull off that role. You really have to know what you are doing, even though I wasn't flying around and doing all these technical feats. You can't have a young physicality to step into that role. It was really mind-driven and experience-driven and knowledge-driven.

Another piece that fascinates me is *Electronics,* and I can only imagine what it was like. It was very avant-garde and before its time. How did audiences respond to it in 1961?

Yes, I think it was terrifically ahead of its time. It had an electronic score, and at that time to have an electronic score not only published but performed at one of the most sophisticated cultural institutions in the world, the New York City Ballet, was news, if not history. It was a fascinating work.

What happened to the piece? It didn't stay around very long.

The reason it didn't prevail is that Balanchine pulled it from the repertoire, because when they did the electronics in the score, it wasn't fully accurate. You cannot be musically inaccurate and keep the fascination of a Balanchine ballet. I think he thought it was a wonderful experiment, but it couldn't be repeated.

Was your role in *Electronics* enjoyable to dance?

We did it only one season, and I believe we did it on the West Coast. I was still too young to have full comprehension and knowledge, and I still didn't know how to fully develop a role, but it was a unique experience. I would do anything to work with Balanchine. It has a very peculiar style and I had never heard electronic music before.

I would like to discuss the black jazz influences on Mr. Balanchine's choreography. The freedom in the pelvis was such a departure from the old masters who choreographed so rigidly.

What a breakthrough when you think about going from the Romantic style of *Giselle* to the grand Imperial style of the Russians, and then the next major statement was Balanchine with tremendous pelvic thrust and tremendous bending at the waist, and passing through balance instead of achieving and staying up on balance. This idea of arriving at balance from an angle and getting up on it and passing through it and extending the gesture instead of just getting straight up and on the balance and coming down from it—you see that in the early works. You see it in *Apollo,* you see it in *Prodigal Son,* you see it in *Orpheus,* and you see it throughout. So where that came from, we would have to say that it was jazz-oriented.

Where do you think those influences came from?

Where and how he arrived at all of that, I certainly don't know, but I know he loved Fred Astaire and he loved and understood jazz and he could dance it. He was really something; he was a fabulous dancer. He used to talk about his conversations with black musicians and about the "shag." He had tremendous background and knowledge, and he always investigated and he was constantly absorbing. To this day how he prepared for his ballets is still a mystery to me.

He crafted an abundant body of work, and the variety in the work is astonishing to me. And it was all quite wonderful.

As much as you can say he used similar devices like pelvic thrusts and the turning of the leg and the flexing of the foot, he always revealed something. He always showed you something new and fresh. He always revealed. He was just revelatory. In his ballets, even though there are certain motifs that are similar and used as devices, there isn't one thing that is the same. Every ballet is different. It's startling. Startling.

What was it like for you the night you received twenty-two encores while dancing at the Bolshoi? What was that evening like?

It was stunning. I was absolutely stunned. I never had an experience like that, and the company to my knowledge has never had a history of an encore before or since. I was totally unprepared as a New York City Ballet dancer and totally unprepared just as a dancer. I really was stunned. It was also Russia, in the middle of the Cuban missile crisis, and it was an oddity. I didn't expect it, and when it happened, I had goose bumps and I was just pouring sweat.

I remember being in a daze and going in and out of the wings, and looking down at the conductor who was making gestures to me. It was a cacophony that had an eye in the middle of the storm, which was me. I was wide-eyed and didn't know what to do. Finally, the conductor made this grandiose gesture and said, "Go back and do it." So I went back onstage and danced it again.

Did the energies in the theatre that night spur you on?

The adrenaline goes to the top, and I went out and danced it again. It was bittersweet because I hadn't pleased Balanchine by doing it. He wasn't pleased at all.

Why do you think that was? Was he uncomfortable with your fame?

I think this was a company that didn't have that kind of precedent, and for me to set it, I guess you could look at it as being arrogant and going against tradition. I established my own precedent. This might have been one part of it. I don't know about Balanchine, and all I can do is surmise and perceive. But it was his first big return since he left Russia, so it had to have been very emotional for him to bring this contemporary neoclassicism to the so-called home of classicism. I think there is a story that one of the Russian officials said to him, "Welcome back to the home of classicism." Balanchine replied, "The home of classicism is no longer Russia."

But Edward, your curtain calls were a tribute to his work. I would think he would be thrilled since it reflected *his* artistry.

Yes, but there were other factors. Not only was this his return to Russia and he was concerned about how his choreography and his company would be accepted, but at the time he focused on Allegra Kent. I am sure it passed his mind that she would have this wonderful success because she was his inspiration at the time. I had a particularly terrific success; so did Arthur Mitchell. Mitchell didn't have the level of my success, but it was comparable. Balanchine made a snide remark about "the people's premiere danseur."

Was that remark meant for you?

I am not sure if it was about Arthur or me. He was not pleased when I had a tremendous success in *Prodigal Son*. He was not

pleased about that. He didn't want to bring *Prodigal.* He first announced it and then he took it off the program. I spoke to him and
told him I had nothing to dance and asked why I was going to Russia.
I was very difficult, and just to shut me up, he said, "OK. All right. You
can have it." Then, when I had a really big success with it, I am not
sure he was pleased. It was a very awkward time for me. I wasn't taking his class and there were a lot of circumstances that could have
contributed to the discomfort.

Was he a difficult man to speak with?

No and yes. He was open and a raconteur and he was charming,
but he also kept you in your place. He certainly kept me in my place.
He kept you always a little off balance. I didn't know if he did that, or
if that was just me being in awe and intimidated and never knowing
what to say to him. I was always feeling like I would say the wrong
thing, and eventually I would, or I would speak my mind, which was
sometimes the wrong thing.

**As you spent more time dancing for him and felt more comfort-
able with the company, did those feelings continue?**

Yes. It prevailed. He once introduced me in Milan at a Gucci store
as "Villella, premiere danseur." But also "Mafioso." I just wonder how
apt that remark was in relation to his conception of me.

Maybe he thought it was amusing.

I am not sure it was a joke. I am sure he was relating to me as a
snot-nosed, smart-ass, tough kid from Queens who didn't have anything but the rough edges and really didn't know how to behave. And
he proved I couldn't behave by denying him and not taking his class.
It was a complicated situation.

Do you regret your decision not to take his class?

I regretted it when it was happening. I knew what was going to happen when I started not to take his class anymore and I started to work
with Stanley. I knew there would be consequences. But the question
was, where were the most dire consequences—in taking his class or
not taking his class and taking Williams's class? In taking Williams's

class, I lived to dance another day. My musculature was in such a state of chaos and disarray that I think if I had kept on the way I was, I don't think I would have lasted more than a couple of years.

You really didn't have a choice.

I felt that I didn't. I discussed it with him and he gave me a pat on the head, and he said, "Not to worry about it." To this day, I feel like I offended him by not taking his class.

I know he wasn't someone who lavished praise, yet there were times when he told you how well you danced. Over the years, it must have been frustrating for you. How did you gauge your work for yourself?

That was his manner and his style. You kind of understood if you pleased him or not. After a certain point, you knew how well you did or didn't because you finally understood what his choreographic demands were, and so we all eventually had a sense of how we should be and how we should dance and what the level of acceptance of "good" was in his eyes.

You speak of knowing when you were "overdancing" as well as when you were right there in the dance. I was talking with a friend of mine, Mikko Nissinen (now the artistic director for Alberta Ballet), and he was talking about his performing experiences. He talked about "holding back with an audience" when he was dancing, how exciting that was for him, and the tremendous interchange of energies between performer and audience.

You don't want to dance at one level the entire evening. You don't want to be full throttle the whole evening because the audience can't differentiate between the shadings. It's like looking at a picture with one bright color dominating. That's the palette: one bright color. You want all of the shadings and all of the support for the proper moment, so you have to shade the energy in the attack, and how you attack.

It's critical not to overdance, but you have to know when to hold back and how much to hold back and not let it fully go. This idea of holding back and keeping it controlled is another enticing aspect for an audience. They may not be able to describe it, but it's enticing for them, that there is abandon and yet it is fully controlled. It's a very exciting thing to watch, rather than something that is very stifled and practiced and predictable.

Does that ability come with age and experience?

Probably. There are some people who have those instincts and those abilities naturally, but it does take understanding and knowledge and exploration and figuring it out. Maybe it takes a day or two, or maybe it takes years, but there is a process to that.

Was there a palpable energy in the audience in terms of the manner in which the audience would respond? Could you tell after dancing for a few minutes what kind of audience you had?

Yes. You can tell inside of a couple minutes what your audience is like for the night. It is one of those crazy intangibles.

How could you tell?

I really couldn't tell you, but you step out onstage and you know whether you are in the presence of a warm, comforting audience, or whether you are in front of a very cold, demanding audience, or a bored audience. It is odd, but you can tell. There is something that comes across those footlights and you understand it. You instinctively adjust your dancing accordingly.

When you were dancing in front of a cold audience, or an audience that is rather removed, would you dance harder and try to go further? How would you shape the performance?

You just seek ways to reach them. You know when you have reached an audience. Then, sometimes you say to yourself, "There is nothing more I can do without being tasteless to reach this audience." You go as far as you can and let it be. You accept it as one of those nights. It happens a lot. Usually, it is opening-night audiences. It's really wild.

You have always been an educator, speaking about ballet since the beginning of your career. Why is the educational aspect so important to you?

First of all, I really like kids. I like young people, and they are fascinating, and sometimes I have the ability to reach them. I can communicate with them. This field has been so wonderful to me, and I would
like everybody to share some of that wonder. We don't have an ongo-
ing process to illuminate the inside of this art form unless we do it.
So we do it. I've done it for the longest time. I think it stems from the
fact that I like kids. I have three kids of my own and I can relate. I
think they keep you honest.

You can't lie to them.

No, you can't talk down to them and you can't talk above their
heads. You have to be able to talk directly to them. I think that there
are two things that they are comfortable with—honesty and quality—
and they inherently understand those things. If you are providing that,
they feel comfortable with you. They really keep you honest. You have
to be very professional with them. I love that in many ways. I like the
spontaneity of kids. Kids should be kids, and sometimes we force
them to behave in a way they are not prepared for. That's why I like
the special programs we do for kids, because they are surrounded by
their peers.

**When you are talking about a ballet, what do you tell people to
look for?**

It depends. If I am in a dance talk or a preperformance talk, I will
try to give them a little bit of a road map to follow. For instance, in
Agon I will suggest that they watch how the music supports everything, and they will see the music in a very different way. George Balanchine has architecturally provided you with the score. His invention
is full of sculptural invention and stylistic invention. Mostly, I like to
give people a sense of relief when they walk into a stark, abstract
work. There are no costumes, and the music is odd and it's atonal
and they can't reference it.

**It's an educational process actually for both the eye and the
mind.**

It's truly an educational process, but it's not that different from football. The more you watch football, the more you understand and see its complications and its intricacies. It's full of people faking one way and trying to make people misunderstand, and it's choreographed. It's full of timings, and you only know it when you fully know it.

What is your opinion of the dance world at present in terms of classical choreographers making work?

We don't have many classical choreographers. But we have an awful lot of modern and alternative choreographers who are people who maybe don't have a certain level of the genius of Balanchine—one wouldn't expect that. There is a lot of mediocrity around. A lot of mediocrity is highly praised and highly funded and highly supported. It confuses me because I am much more interested in master work.

We have very few classical choreographers who are developing in relation to other fields and in relation to audiences and budgets. Classical companies are seeking other choreographers to create work for them. I think that works in rare cases. I don't think that fully works.

Why not?

I don't think that modern choreographers are necessarily capable of choreographing on classical people. I don't think that classical people are necessarily educated to articulate modern dance, the style, manner, and approach. In certain areas, it works very well. Paul Taylor in a lot of his work has a classical sensibility. I think Mark Morris is a choreographer who has a lot of classical sensibility as well.

And the classical form will suffer because there is that void.

Classicism is in very difficult shape, and the two great classical choreographers, Balanchine and Robbins, are no longer with us. Those men were the two providers of manner, style, development, evolution, and extension of the classical and traditional line. We are not producing a follow-up to that. At Miami City Ballet, we are holding choreographic workshops whereby a fledgling choreographer can study the components. They have to adhere to certain demands, get two or three pieces of music to digest and break down the score, and articulate the elements that they wish to develop. They will also break down the elements by studying master work from Bournonville, Petipa, and Balanchine.

What do you think about choreographers' abilities to pass on their talents, and how can they do that?

What worries me is that we have a plethora of choreographers. We have modern dance, ethnic dance, all kinds of theatricalized dance. We have few classical choreographers left. Classical choreography by its nature, by its vocabulary and its structures and forms, has so many more elements that need to be known and adhered to. There is a tremendous learning process to become a classical choreographer. You have to choreograph in that field to find your voice. But if the funders are telling you to make breakthrough work, how can you do that when you haven't gotten your foundation yet? You have to go through this process just as Picasso went through a series of stages before he found his full voice.

I'd like to discuss your own choreography. It must be difficult to find time to do that given your responsibilities.

I think that choreographing is a full-time profession. Certainly if you are not on the level of some of the people we have talked about and you don't have that broad, phenomenal, instinctive talent, you have to really, really work at this. You have to make a decision. There is no way I could call myself a full-time choreographer and be both the founding artistic director of the organization and the executive director. There aren't enough hours in the day. I have a lot of energy, but I don't have that much energy.

Would you like to spend more time choreographing?

I would like to explore it more. I keep trying to set up circumstances so that I can do that, but it's mostly finding the time to do the investigation, the exploration, the research, and the preproduction stuff. Getting into production and putting steps to music is complicated, but not nearly as time-consuming as organizing and preparing, because you should not be listening to four notes and putting a step to it. You have to have some point of departure. You have to structure the work and form it.

It's like writing a play. You have to know what's going into the first act, and how you are going to close it. And ask yourself, "Who are these people on stage and where do they come from? How do they behave? How do they relate to each other? What does the music mean? What can you expose about the music that is so unique?" These are all questions that you have to answer before you think about making a step. That takes time and investigation. You have to listen. You have to read and look. I have made a few pieces for the company, but I am a director who would like to put some steps to music every now and again.

Do you have notes and ideas tucked away for the future?

Sure. One of the things I would like to explore is rhythms and to do a work based on rhythm. When I teach class, I am very rhythm-driven, because I want our dancers to be aware of not just an eight-bar phrase but what's going on between the counts in those eight bars. Is it and one, two, three, four, AND one? Or is it ONE, TWO, THREE, FOUR? Or is it one AND two AND three and four? It depends on what you are going to do within a certain distance measured by time and how you subdivide that and where you put accents in a logical, practical way that relates to music and dance. That would be fun.

"Who are these people?" "Are they just rhythm maniacs?" I have to find some period and reason for these people to be together and why they relate to each other and what the rhythms mean. That's what takes time, to have legitimate reasons to put steps to music. You have to justify it all, artfully.

Can you give me some background on *Narkissos*? What was your impetus to make that work?

I read a short play by my agent's husband, and it was a contemporary rendition of *Narcissus*. I did it as a play with movement, a segment of it at the Actor's Studio with a director. Then somebody recommended Robert Prince to do the music, and that was my first mistake since I had never worked with a composer before. I thought you agreed to a certain time and that a certain amount of material would be delivered and you proceeded from there. If I had more experience, what I would have done is have the score done in the first year and begun choreographing at the end of the second year so that I would have time to digest it. But I didn't have experience, and you pay for those things. You think you know what to do until you start doing it.

Can you tell me about the evolution of your first ballet, *Shenandoah*?

I was asked to do a piece with the New York Philharmonic and André Kostelanetz. They were always looking for off-beat kinds of stuff. At that time, my agent, Janet Roberts, who was my dearest and closest friend, knew a guy who was a folk singer, and he was interested in sea shanties. I talked to him about doing something with the Philharmonic. I began to put together these little pieces to make something of a segment for an evening for the Philharmonic, and one of them was *Shenandoah*. I used it for that occasion and began to use it as a concert piece. Later on, I did a ballet for the New Jersey Ballet based on the sea shanties. . . . It's a little piece that developed into a half-hour ballet.

What do you imagine the future of dance to be?

It is really hard to say because normally what happens is a choreographer comes along and begins to show you the way. You can count them almost on one hand: Bournonville, Petipa, Fokine, Balanchine, Robbins, Ashton. In 150 years, it is only six or eight choreographers. They are the ones who basically make the statement, and then you teach accordingly to come up to where they have taken classical choreography.

That's the normal process. We have to be patient. It is like having a bridge between the giants right now. There is no major, major choreographer working today on that level. It's not to say there aren't any good choreographers working, but not people who are that prolific and can change the face of an art form. We have to be patient, and in the interim, prepare. That's why I think it is critical that we prepare around Balanchine because that was the last major, choreographic, and technical statement that has been made.

2

Merce Cunningham

"Merce Cunningham and John Cage presented a program of solo dances and of percussionist music last night which was of the greatest esthetic elegance. The audience, an intelligent one, enjoyed and applauded.

It was Mr. Cunningham's first solo recital, though he is well known to dance audiences as soloist in Martha Graham's company. His gifts as a lyric dancer are most remarkable. His build resembles that of the juvenile saltimbanques of the early Picasso canvases. As a dancer his instep and his knees are extraordinarily elastic and quick; his steps, runs, knee bends, and leaps are brilliant in lightness and speed. His torso can turn on its vertical axis with great sensitivity, his shoulders are held lightly free, and his head poises intelligently. The arms are light and long, they float. . . .

"His dances are built on the rhythm of a body in movement, and on its irregular phrase lengths. And the perfection with which he can indicate the rise and fall of an impulse gives one an esthetic pleasure of exceptional delicacy."

————**Edwin Denby, *Looking at the Dance (Elegance in Isolation)*, 1944**

Imagine for a moment that it is the 1940s, and you are inside a
small dance studio in New York City. The dancers practicing at the
barre are part of Martha Graham's company. You are not the only
one observing the rehearsal, however. There is another person there
who is a frequent guest of Ms. Graham's. Intuitively, this guest is
able to focus her attention on the dancers' feet, although she cannot actually see the dancers.

Through sign language, she asks Graham, "What is jumping?",
for she does not understand the concept. Graham leads her to the
barre where a male dancer is standing and gently places the
woman's hands on his waist. She tells him gently, "Be very careful.
I'm putting her hands on your body." Then the dancer jumps into
the air in first position while the woman's hands softly tuck around
his waist like Velcro. All eyes in the studio follow this demonstration, and they watch intently as the woman's facial expression
changes from curiosity to joy.

In her autobiography, *Blood Memory,* Graham wrote of that
moment, "You could see the enthusiasm in her mind as she threw
her arms in the air and exclaimed, 'How like thought. How like the
mind it is.'"

The blind woman was Helen Keller. The dancer, Merce
Cunningham.

How revelatory that Graham would choose the young Cunningham to be Keller's guide into learning another language: the language of the dancer. In that brief encounter Keller sought to
uncover the truth, the truth of the body. That truth has always been
Cunningham's gospel.

Merce Cunningham has always been a truth-seeker. Fiercely
committed to extending the boundaries of the human form, Cunningham is a maverick, using "chance" methods from the ancient
Chinese oracle, the I-Ching, as a tool for movement exploration,
and, in recent years, employing computer-assisted technology called
LIFEFORMS. He told me, "LIFEFORMS has opened up my mind
about making steps so I can see all kinds of possibilities, not necessarily do them, see all kinds of possibilities which were always
there, but I didn't see them."

Merce Cunningham, *The Chair Solo*. Copyright 1995 by Jed Downhill.

Cunningham liberated modern dance by shredding the rules for performance and its integral components: music, lighting, costumes, stage design, and performance space. All of the various elements of the performance function as self-contained entities, since Cunningham long ago dispensed with narrative and "matching" music. Even the manner in which a Cunningham dancer is trained is based on his ceaseless and personal exploration of movement. Now in his eighth decade, he continues to open the doors to a myriad of possibilities for dance.

His choreography possesses its own rhythmic structure and "coincides" with the music and the decor, instead of reflecting them. With artist John Cage (until his death), musical director and ally, Cunningham shared a vision to present all of the aspects of performance in a new manner, revolutionizing the art form. Their dedication has not only educated audiences worldwide but permanently changed our perceptions of what dance and performance is and what it can be.

Growing up in Centralia, Washington, Cunningham's dance teacher Maude Barrett recognized his talents, and, at age fifteen, he began his performing career in not-quite-up-to-par clubs with Barrett's younger daughter, Marjorie. Cunningham explained: "We had an act. Each of us did a solo and we had a duet, some kind of soft-shoe number that Mrs. Barrett had arranged. Eventually, we did exhibition ballroom together in rather shoddy clubs. I think I knew then *this* is what I wanted to do. I was possessed by it."

He briefly attended George Washington University, but his passion led him to transfer his studies to the Cornish School of Fine and Applied Arts. During a summer session at Mills College in Oakland, California (while he was attending a dance residency), Cunningham was handpicked by Martha Graham, the doyenne of modern dance, to join her company in New York City. While he was in the company, he appeared in many of her signature pieces, performing the roles of the Revivalist in *Appalachian Spring*, the Acrobat in *Every Soul Is a Circus*, and the Christ figure in *El Penitente*.

However, every extraordinary life usually must choose whether or not to honor the vision, the "ideal" that speaks to each alone, and Cunningham was no exception. Although he co-choreographed works with fellow Graham dancer Jean Erdman during the 1940s, he was restless to find his own way, and he decided to leave Graham's company.

Teaching his unique and evolving gestural language in a cold-water apartment in New York (at first with only one student), Cunningham refused to abandon his ideas for performance. His collaborations with Cage were on the cutting edge; they were controversial and frequently sparked debate in the artistic community. He was both vilified and praised, but he continued to work even when audiences departed and the critics ignored him. But those days are long gone, and as Nancy Dalva wrote in *The Daily Texan,* "Cunningham has not gone establishment, but the establishment has gone Cunningham."

Many of his most devoted audience members were composed of painters, sculptors, and other artists who often became his benefactors during times of financial duress. When the company was invited to perform at the Paris International Dance Festival in 1966, the United States government refused to fund the trip. But the company did perform in France with the donation of funds from the proceeds of a sale of a Joan Miró painting arranged by a patron.

No doubt one of the reasons that so many avant-garde artists were attracted to Cunningham's and Cage's work was the fact that both men not only honored the separation of music, costumes, and lighting from the dance but each element shared top billing and was not subordinate, offering artists in their respective fields the opportunity to explore and follow their own visions without interference. Those freedoms were enticing to Jasper Johns, Robert Rauschenberg, Frank Stella, and Remy Charlip.

The enigmatic manner in which he creates his "steps" is intriguing. He won't speak about the "meaning" of the works since he "doesn't want to impose," leaving us to our own interpretation. Through the years, Cunningham continues to use one of the world's oldest and most profound divination systems, the I-Ching, in tandem with exploring and choosing movement possibilities. Relying on dice (and, in the past, pennies), he employs the dice for the creation, order, and construction of movements. Paradoxically, this procedure is both liberating and constrictive, but he navigates like a Zen master with total faith. That surrender to the artistic process is not haphazard but a carefully articulated trust that there are deeper universal forces that he can tap into.

His enduring confidence in that method speaks volumes about the mysteries of the creative process. I imagine him wrestling with many blueprints of movement, endlessly calculating, observing, and listening for what he needs, journeying from order to disorder and back again, from formlessness to form to offer us physical poetry.

The Herculean abilities of his dancers, not to mention their fearlessness in performing to music that they often have never heard, requires an extraordinary intelligence, both intellectual and physical. The lyrical strength of the company members, especially when they hold their stance in inordinately sustained movements with total focus, never ceases to amaze me. When I watch a Cunningham piece, sometimes I believe I am watching the motion of a Calder sculpture or sitting in a garden after a heavy rain when everything is lush. As a result, many of the dancers' haunting and beautiful images remain in my mind's eye for days.

Although, there are literally hundreds of descriptions of Cunningham's works, one of my favorites is by Sybil Sheaver written in the 1940s and still applicable almost sixty years later. "Today, one has to transport oneself into Cunningham's world as though you were listening to the language of animals or insects. I like his work best because it is pure, and once you have made that transition to his world, you can see that."

The willingness to "be transported" is key to obtaining the full sensory pleasures of a Cunningham concert. Leading us into uncharted territory, he offers us the opportunity to receive dance in a new way, and his work rewards both the eye and the ear if one is fully attentive and has an open mind. Cunningham's innovative use of space, decor, and rhythm in tandem with music that can easily soothe or assault actually gives us freedom, freedom for our eyes to wander where they wish, and freedom from any preconceived notions about what we are hearing and seeing. One is just never sure what will happen next.

Who else besides Cunningham would create Events: virtual non-stop, nonsequential performance in which dancers perform segments of previous repertoire strung together with no apparent theme while they move to music that they have never heard before. All elements of the familiar are removed. I have always respected how brave the dancers are to abandon themselves fully and entirely to the movement. From the standpoint of the dancer, it's a surrender from fear to physical trust. If you have seen one Event, you have not seen them all.

When I was preparing for my meeting with Cunningham, I wasn't sure how to narrow down the huge caché of questions that I had prepared. I decided to use the I-Ching to make the final selection of the questions. I spent hours methodically throwing my pennies and recording, deleting, and numbering each of the questions from my list. Before our interview in Southern California, I explained to him how I chose my questions. He seemed genuinely delighted that I used "chance" and assured me that they were indeed the "right" questions. Although the questions do not follow a particular theme, I took pains to follow the I-Ching–assisted questions whenever I could. However, that didn't stop the flow of conversation.

We sat in the seats of an old theatre hall where Cunningham's company was practicing for their performance that evening. Although, there were a lot of people coordinating the myriad activities for opening night, and the stagehands, lighting technicians, and others moved in a swarm around us, he seemed engrossed in the pleasures of watching the dancers. While we spoke, he glanced approvingly at the company members and told me how pleased he was just to watch *movement*.

In 1947, you created *The Seasons* at the beginning of your choreographic career for the Ballet Society (the precursor to the New York City Ballet), and I am interested in knowing more about how that piece came about.

Lincoln Kirstein, who sponsored the Ballet Society, invited me to make a work for their first season with John Cage as composer. Originally, I wanted Morris Graves to do the decor for it since, in my mind, it concerned the atmosphere of the Northwest where both Cage and I had been. But Morris didn't want to do it, and I could tell he didn't care to work under union restrictions, so Lincoln arranged for Isamu Noguchi to do the decor. That is how it began. I went to the American Ballet School to choose the dancers.

Tanaquil Le Clercq was in it, too. From what I have read about her, she was an extraordinary dancer, and she really interests me.

Yes, she was in it. She was a very beautiful dancer, special, and I enjoyed working with her very much.

What made her so special as a dancer?

I thought her physical look was extraordinary. She was quite a tall person, slender of course, with a long, beautiful, oval face. She was young; she must have been seventeen years old at that time. I enjoyed working with her, dancing with her, and my memories are that she was gifted and, working with me, agreeable and not difficult. When a movement that was not familiar to her within the ballet came up and was strange to her, she would ask how to do it. We would work at it. The first performance was given in the Ziegfeld Theatre. It was a handsome Broadway house, a good stage.

What were you like as a child? Did you have any sense that you would dance at an early age?

I wouldn't have verbalized it then, of course, but I always wanted to be in the theatre. I don't know how else to explain that. There is nothing in my family that would have led to this.

Did your family take you to the theatre?

Yes. I remember movies, of course. But I have a vague memory—I would have been, perhaps, five, six, or seven years old—of going to the local theatre to see vaudeville (it was still going on). My father liked going to the theatre. He didn't go often, but he enjoyed it. He was a lawyer.

In my adolescent years I took tap dancing with this wonderful woman, Mrs. Maude Barrett, a marvelous person. She was so full of energy and had been in every form of theatre, vaudeville, nightclubs, the circus. She taught tap dances and eventually, when I was fifteen, her daughter Marjorie and I performed together. We had an act. Each of us did a solo and then we had a duet—some kind of soft-shoe number that Mrs. Barrett had arranged. Eventually, we did ballroom exhibition together in rather shoddy clubs, really shoddy in memory, but still we did it. I think I knew by then, whatever else, *this* is what I wanted to do. I'm intellectualizing it all now, but then I was simply possessed by it.

That's a nice way to put it.

There wasn't anything else. I didn't particularly like sports. I couldn't imagine doing anything else. When I would try something else, it didn't seem of interest at all. But when I did *this,* that was clearly it.

Did your family foster your artistic needs?

They were helpful, and they didn't get in the way. My mother was probably upset by the whole thing, but my father's principle was that "you should do what you wanted to as long as you worked at it." He was a liberal man that way. I remember he was talking to the three of us, my brothers and myself, and he said clearly, "I don't care what you do as long as you work at it." As long as you don't slough off, in other words, and he didn't mean eight hours a day necessarily, but if you are involved in something, *Do it!* Because he was involved in law, and that, I must say, caught me—not the law, but his involvement in it. I never forgot that, his incredible concentration and interest in it.

In the book, *The Impermanent Art*, you said, "If the dancer dances, everything is there." Can you elaborate on that statement? Are you talking about passion?

Absolute passion, passion for movement. I think I must have had that always, and again, I wouldn't have verbalized it. I still have it. It's extraordinary to me the things I can still see and know about. That's the part that touches me deeply. I think everyone could see it in the dancing of Fred Astaire. Here was this extraordinary, and in a way, funny-looking man. Who cared? But his dancing touched everybody. As my father said, "He sure could dance," and it was not just technical skill. He was skilled, Lord knows, and worked hard at it, but it's beyond that.

Did you ever meet him?

No. I just admired him enormously. You see, he was the person I saw dance in the movies, and I thought he was fantastic. There were others of course—the wonderful Bill Robinson with Shirley Temple, "The Nicholas Brothers," but it was Astaire who struck me.

I work with camera, you know, and people say to me, "On camera, dancing doesn't work as well as on the stage." I always say, "Almost all of the people who saw Fred Astaire dance only saw him on film. They didn't see him onstage." He was on the stage, certainly, but our experience of him was through film.

Did you watch all of his films?

I am sure I have seen them all. But I don't think of skill with Astaire, that isn't what comes up, although he was unbelievably skilled. But it was just his plain passion for dancing. I am sure that is why he struck so many viewers who saw him. It wasn't as though he was trying to show you how good he was. It was clearly that this man was doing what he could do in this astonishing way and with this manner that allowed you to see the freedom with which he could dance. But the skill was also there.

Do you think that dancers are born dancers?

I think it is different. Some people are gifted in ways more than others. Sometimes the gifts are in one direction, sometimes in another, and sometimes they aren't really gifts for dancing. But people are struck by it, and they want to do it, and they work at it, and they can become dancers. But there is a kind of *instinct* about dancing; I don't know any other word.

I think one of the reasons it can fascinate intellectuals is that it lies between the instinctual part of our nature and the intellectual. But it remains primarily in the instinctual; it has something of the quality of an animal. I don't mean necessarily a wild animal. For example, I watch dancers learning steps, and with some of them, they must be told very clearly from the start "Is it the right foot?" "Are you turned out?" They have to be told the exact placement of the arm before they attempt to do it. It doesn't mean they can't do it; they eventually may do it very well. But other dancers "see" it; they will start to move, and they don't have to ask questions. They just absorb it through the skin. It is marvelous to watch.

It would be wonderful to have that gift.

If I have any gift, that's it. I can absorb movement by looking at it. One wants to be precise, but you absorb it and then you go back and work at it. Very often the ones who do this will absorb the movement and then they realize without any words that they are on the wrong foot, so they shift balance. They don't have to ask any questions.

What you are talking about is a visceral intelligence.

It is. It's visceral, it's very kinesthetic—the ability to absorb something the way animals can. I think it is one of the moments for a dancer that makes something marvelous to see.

Merce, do you miss dancing?

I still dance by myself. Yes. It's been my life. I am trying to think how to say this. I want to eat up my dance experience regardless of age and physical infirmities. I do it in private, by myself. There is a phrase in Westbeth, our studio in New York, "Merce's five minutes." After the daily rehearsal, when the company is finished, and before the class has to come in, there is "Merce's five minutes." I dance by myself at the barre. It's what I do, and I do it in private. On the other hand, to eat it up in public is more outrageous.

Can you tell me how you feel when you are onstage? I have seen you, and you have such an incredible presence.

I love being onstage. It's home for me, and somehow it has always been home. I don't know if it's ego, probably it is that, but it is also something more than that. It's like you become a larger being somehow.

Maybe it is the element of risk that is involved, but I don't think it's just ego. The stage allows one to be something else that touches me.

Do you think there is a difference between "you" the man and "you" the performer?

Not so much. I don't think so. I like very much making up steps. It's not a question of good or bad. Someone else might like to make cakes or grow a garden or direct a film. I like to make steps.

Does it come easily to you?

Yes, most of the time.

Has it always been that way for you?

No, no, but perhaps it was. Curiously enough, this technology with which I work now, the dance computer program called LIFEFORMS, has opened my mind about making steps so I can see all kinds of possibilities, not necessarily do them, but see possibilities that were always there, that I didn't catch previously.

You are a pioneer in so many areas and you have been able to teach people to see movement in a different way.

I think movement is so fascinating. I never can understand why people feel there should be something behind it. I understand that you can think that way to try to have a meaning or a reference point. I know you can do that, but for me it really is what it is. I watch those two up there (some of the dancers who are practicing at the barre), and even though they are doing their warm-up exercises, it is still fascinating to me.

Do you consider yourself an educator?

No. I have to teach, but I do not enjoy it.

Why?

Because so much of it has to be repetitive. It has to be for the dancer to physically train the body to be responsive. You have students who can see movement and then they think they know it, but they don't know it physically. I always had to teach a great deal for

Merce Cunningham in *Changeling,* 1956. *Copyright 1956 by Richard Rutledge. Reproduced by permission of Merce Cunningham Dance Foundation.*

survival, and often I would have people in the class who were totally hopeless as possible dancers.

I remember a young guy who was in his twenties, was clearly bright, and he was sure he was physically gifted. He was in an elementary class. I always demonstrate an exercise three times at least. They see it for the first time, they maybe get it the second time, and then I would reinforce via a third showing. I could see he saw it; he muttered, "I've got it" after the second showing, and then when I did the third repeat, he was simply irritated. We started and he was physically like a hopeless idiot, and he couldn't get from one foot to the other, could not understand why, since he saw it through the eye and he couldn't do it. He thought I hadn't shown it clearly, but he was a bright guy and realized it was in his lap. He had the mental capacity to see, but the not the physical capacity to translate. I see it often in classes, as many teachers do.

That must be very frustrating for both student and teacher.

Yes, that part, but there is a great deal of necessary repetition. It is essential, otherwise the stretch of the physical image doesn't happen. People may see it in their heads, but they cannot always do it.

Merce, do you find that your dreams influence pictures of movement for you, or your ideas about movement?

I don't think of dreams as much of an influence. I think of things I see, perhaps an odd movement a person does. I remember one man crossing a street; he must have been a tourist in New York. He couldn't decide whether to start or stop because other people were jaywalking. He would step off the curb and then back on it, back and forth, and the shifting seemed to take a long time. Then, finally he got into the street, and by that time the lights changed, so he had to run. I thought, "That's moving!" The world is full of movement, and that is what interests me.

I noticed you drawing at the hotel. What do you usually sketch?

I draw all sorts of things, animals, birds. I enjoy it greatly. It takes one's concentration, takes one's mind off of one's troubles because one can pay attention to the details. It is difficult to get up in the morning and start bending over, so I sit down with tea and make a drawing, and that way my mind is somewhere else.

Does the artwork influence you?

Oh, of course, I am sure it has. I don't do it with that in mind; I just do it to make drawings.

Have you ever had a show of your work?

Yes. One or two in a New York gallery that handles my work. The person I work with is Margarete Roeder. She is a lovely person and generous to show them.

Do you use Laban notation or Benesh notation?

No. I have developed a notation of my own, but that is only because it is practical and it doesn't answer the purpose of it. I think that LIFEFORMS, in any event a technical notation, is a major step toward a visual notation. There is no question, but it will take a while because of the technological advances in recording movement. Even with my limited awareness of LIFEFORMS, I can see how useful it is becoming for notating motion, and for being clear about what a movement is. There are all kinds of glitches and problems which are simply technical, and it is expensive to work with, so it will take a long time, but that's where we will be.

Most choreographers don't use that type of technology yet.

There isn't access, and there is fear about technology. I have been lucky about access. I just decided I didn't know anything about it, so I could be stupid. I am not frightened. So I go ahead and fumble and make mistakes, but nobody cares and I have the experience.

And, that's the only way to learn.

Yes. It is marvelously open. It's difficult, not easy fumbling around, and I don't have a great deal of time to spend with it because I am working with the dancers. But I can put phrases into the computer memory and can bring them back for future use. I make notes, utilizing various shorthand forms I have evolved. Chris Komar, who was with me for a number of years, furthered my primitive notation. Naturally, as with any dance company, we have videos of a great many of the works.

Do you go back to watch pieces that you did twenty-five or thirty years ago?

Only if it needs to be checked, if we are reviving it.

Would you change anything?

No, I don't, unless for practical reasons; for example, a new dancer who is replacing someone and a movement doesn't work for him or her. I don't shift it radically; I don't see the point to that. I just think the dances should as much as possible be what they were.

If a dancer were having difficulties, would you alter it?

I could help the dancer with that and shift it to work for that partic- ular individual. That I would do.

But maintaining the integrity of that particular movement?

Yes, and the rhythm of it, where it is in the phrasing, yes. But each person is different and the skill varies. Someone can do something a certain way, a different dancer in another way. I don't mind changing.

When you hire a dancer to be in the company, what qualities do you look for?

They don't audition. We have class and they come to that. That's the only way I have ever done it. If someone comes to the studio who is interested in working with us, we ask them to take a class. I think it's fairer than an audition; I can watch them over a period of time and they can also begin to know what the situation is, not just the technique, but also what's involved in the thinking. On occasion, only twice I remember, have there been dancers who were good ones, but they couldn't deal with the way we work. I would have been happy to have them.

What do you mean?

Well, I work in a way that's not to music. I remember one dancer who was really very good but he simply said he was sorry, he couldn't deal with that. He needed the music. I understood. He had attended classes briefly, and he was a good dancer, and I was sorry to lose him. Sometimes, too, a dancer can't deal with the way we rehearse. We work in silence, without the music, and the dancer has to find a way to make the phrase work individually. I help, certainly, but each one needs to find a way to do a given phrase or movement.

Most dancers are used to be told precisely, "Now, this is what you do, or you should do it like that person is doing it," that form of imitation. I never liked that and have tried to avoid it. I don't object to another working in that way, but it is not my way. I would prefer to work in a way that as much as possible allows the dancer to discover the phrase or movement from herself or himself.

So there's freedom.

It's both precise and free at the same time. I will tell you a story. We have a long work called *Ocean* which lasts an hour and a half. We hadn't rehearsed it since we did it at Lincoln Center about six months ago. I thought we should go through it because we were going to do it in Japan. Six months, remember. There is one new dancer in it who knew the steps but had never done it with the other dancers, so we started and the new dancer managed quite well. There were some problems, but not huge problems. It's an hour and a half long and they came about twenty-seven seconds too fast.

That's marvelous.

That's the kind of memory, physical memory, that all dancers have. Dancers who work with music think that it doesn't exist for them, and it's not true. All dancers have it.

When you are in rehearsal, do the dancers work in silence?

We work in silence, but it's not really silent since the dancers make all these foot sounds and the sounds that are around.

You made a terrific comment about "the meaning of the dance." You said, "I don't want to impose on anyone." Are you saying you don't want to tell people what they need to see? This seems to me a very ego-less position.

I think it is better if people can make up their own minds without someone else having to "tell them." You can show them something. You see, I believe strongly that theatre (and I always include dance in theatre), should be a situation where you could have an experience that you never had before, so that rather than being told ahead of time how you should receive that experience, just go ahead and have it. Afterwards, of course, you can have questions and discussions. That is actually about education and information and that's essential,

Merce Cunningham, Carolyn Brown, and Steve Paxton in *Aeon,* 1961.
Copyright 1961 by Richard Rutledge. Reproduced by permission of Merce
Cunningham Dance Foundation.

but I never liked the premise that you should be told about an art before you look at it or hear it. I think it distorts your experience. It's like trying to explain to someone who has never seen a tree what a tree is, whereas if the person saw one, it becomes part of their experience rather than seeing it through somebody else's eyes.

Merce, do you read reviews?

Almost never. Years ago there were very few, or they were mostly unkind. Then, we, the dance company, went on a world tour and there was a great deal written about us, mainly in languages that I didn't understand, so I thought, "Oh, I don't have to worry."

I always bring up Edwin Denby because he was such a remarkable critic—his perception of dancing and his ability to put it into language in such a plain, direct, and poetic way. I don't think that Edwin liked what I did in my later work, and it mattered to me because of his gifts at looking. He used to attend everything in the dance world, even toward the end of his life. There would be few in the audience for a young dancer's program, one of whom was Edwin. He had a brilliant gift for looking at dance and a humane way of writing about it.

He was able to make the dance performance come alive, and he had such an incredible eye. Can you tell me more about him?

I remember going to programs with him years back, when there were few performances. He invited me to this particular program. We were watching a young dancer who was not particularly good, and Edwin said quietly, "Isn't it interesting with a young dancer how the arm looks long from elbow to hand, and with a more experienced dancer it looks long from shoulder to elbow?" Sometimes I would be sitting with him and he would laugh, and I knew I missed something. I hadn't seen something he had seen.

Would you discuss the performance?

Yes, but, mostly he would talk. I enjoyed listening to him because it was interesting. He was a marvelously civilized man, a wonderful person with humor and intelligence.

In the beginning when people didn't come to your studio to watch your work and the critics didn't attend, what kept you going?

I thought even from the beginning—certainly I didn't intellectualize it the way I am doing now—but I felt the ideas John Cage and I were working with were fascinating. I wasn't sure, never have been, that the way in which I was utilizing the ideas was the only way or the best way, and I could see that another person coming from another angle could see it another way.

I remember one of the solos that I presented on the first program we gave together, back in 1944 for which he [Cage] had composed the music. Although the structure of the dance/music relationship was tighter than now, still the separation of the music and the dance was apparent. In other words, when he made a loud strong sound, I didn't necessarily do a big strong movement. Even then, the feeling of a form of freedom was present. There was such a sense of being precise and free at the same time.

Was it an exhilarating feeling?

Yes. Sometimes through the years it was difficult too. That sense has never left me in my work, as you did with the I-Ching when you asked the questions. That allowance for the mind to be free enough to let something else come in, and then find a way to deal with it.

Isn't it really about giving up control and yet, you don't really, you surrender to the process.

That's right. For that moment, you let the decision come from the moment you are in, the space you are in, and accept that, and find a way to work with it.

Can you give me an example of how you work with the I-Ching in terms of the creation of the dance phrase?

Yes. I can take a simple phrase. Say, you have a run and a jump and a fall, OK? It seems physically logical to run, jump, and fall in that order. But using chance operations, you throw for a decision as to order. Tossing the dice, the order comes up: fall, jump, and run. One thinks one can't do that. But why not? Why can't you do it? Try it out and you can add something to your physical experience outside of the mind's preferences that can enlarge your possibilities. The example is a simple one, of course. But the two personal decisions—"I don't like it" and "I can't do that"— if dropped can open up possibilities.

Have dancers come to you and said, "I can't do this. My body won't do this."?

In the working-out process, sometimes movements have come up that were clearly impossible, but I usually have attempted to try them out (I can work at this by myself, or with the dancers), and in the process discovered some other possibility of which I wasn't aware. You think it won't work that way, but it can work this way. In other words, you have expanded your experience about what is possible. Naturally, there are things you can't do.

In LIFEFORMS, you can turn the head around three times, but we know we can't do that. You can of course, technologically, but it's like a joke or an aberration in some way, because it isn't within the scale of the human body. Sometimes the amount of complexity that I have used has been almost overwhelming. How could I figure to get all of this together in my head and take it to the dancers? I have had to take one layer at a time: what the feet do . . . what the torso does. . . . .

Would you throw the I-Ching specifically to find out the movement for the hands or feet?

It depends on the complexity of the compositional procedure.

Do you have ideas about what you would like to create in the future?

I would like to use different screens, big and little screens all around, huge screens all around you with different dancing or with a collage like an Event. For example, you could watch a screen with a particular Event sequence, using the same material, but each screen would use it in a different way, all to go on at once. To have a screen on the ceiling would add to the mixture.

That would be wild. Your eyes would be dancing all over. Marcel Duchamp spoke a lot about what he called "the fourth dimension." How much of his influence is in your work? I know you were friends with him.

I don't think there are specific things. Of course, the one dance, *Walkaround Time,* was specifically concerned with Duchamp's the *Large Glass.* But it was his way of thinking and being as a person that was extraordinary. And his physical presence. He seemed always to be sitting down and smoking a cigar. People would say, "He isn't doing anything," but he was always busy, I think.

John Cage admired him enormously because of his attitude toward art and what it could be in the twentieth century. It shifted people's ideas of what art is and how it could enter your experience, with the ready-mades, and with the *Large Glass.* After the glass was broken, he didn't say it was wrong; he accepted it.

That's very much the way you work.

Yes. That is a very good example. He simply accepted it and didn't think that he had to remake it.

You said that the "dance was the natural double for metaphysical problems and paradoxes." Can you tell me what you meant by that?

I don't remember saying that; it sounds too intellectual for me. But I don't think it is a substitute for anything. It is what it is, and if you can find a way to enjoy it, that's marvelous, and if you can't, then you really don't have to have anything to do with it. And actually that's what some people do.

Merce, do you worry about the future of dance?

No. I think its going to continue; it's like anything else. Look at the history of the world in the way that things have changed and not changed. Dancing is bound by the fact that we still have two arms and legs and one head, and the torso moves around and has limits, but within those limits, the variety is endless. Absolutely endless as far as I can see.

3

Mark Morris

"There is orchestration throughout. . . . nothing is for itself, but each thing partaking of the other is living it's greatest possibility, is surpassing itself with vitality and meaning and is part of the making of a great unity. So, with the works of the great masters."

———Robert Henri, *The Art Spirit*

When I first saw the Mark Morris Dance Group perform the magnificent *L'Allegro, il Penseroso ed il Moderato,* I wept. I thought then, as I still do, that this piece is one of the most mood-elevating, witty, and joyous choreographic works I have ever seen. But, you don't have to take my word for it. In 1997, the Mark Morris Dance Group received the prestigious Laurence Olivier Award for the work, and in the same year *The London Evening Standard* proclaimed *L'Allegro* the "Outstanding Production of the Year" as part of their Outstanding Ballet and Music Awards program.

L'Allegro bathes audiences in light and is a prayer to the human spirit. It is a reaffirmation to those jaded among us that life can be good indeed. It's a strong work and perhaps one of Morris' finest: romantic, complex, clever, and beautiful. The dancers literally swim in Handel's composition. His trademark use of the ensemble (no star system here) is apparent, and the group's energies seem to be guided by unseen vibrations that bring them together, tear them apart, and back to the circle again in celebration. The architecture of the piece would make for a grand physical mandala.

L'Allegro is alive with choreographic color, rich in musicality, and depicts what a heart and head Morris possesses. It is easy to understand why one critic wrote after attending a performance that she wanted to run up on stage to join the dancers' outstretched hands. That inclination is obvious to anyone who has seen the work.

Morris's talents earned him a MacArthur "genius" grant when he was only 35 years old, an honor usually reserved for artists decades older. He received the Capezio Dance Award in 1997. But his enormous and consistent body of work speaks volumes about his gifts: passion, knowledge of movement, heightened musicality, and a unique choreographic versatility in his dancemaking and performing career. In addition to sitting at the helm of the Mark Morris Dance Group, choreographing and performing, he is cofounder with Mikhail Baryshnikov of The White Oak Dance Project, a small dance ensemble that frequently features Morris's inspired choreography. In 1998, Morris worked on Broadway as choreographer and director for Paul Simon's ill-fated production of *The Capeman.* He also sets work for many dance companies, including the San Francisco

Mark Morris in rehearsal. *Copyright Chantal Regnault. Courtesy of the Mark Morris Dance Group.*

Ballet (which is no mean feat for a modern dance choreographer), and continues to be in perpetual creative motion. His company has a schedule that most companies would covet performing in the States and all over the world, usually to a sold-out crowd.

After extensive study at the dance studio of Verla Flowers in his hometown, Morris performed with the Koleda Folk Ensemble, and later danced with the companies of Lar Lubovitch, Eliot Feld, Laura Dean, and Hanna Kahn before establishing the Mark Morris Dance Group.

When he was 32 years old, he was appointed artistic director in residence for Brussel's Thēâtre Royal de la Monnaie. One might think that newspaper headlines proclaiming "Mark Morris, Go Home!" would have curtailed his artistic sensibilities, but that was not the case. Instead, Morris made two spectacular pieces, *L'Allegro* and the operatic piece *Dido and Aeneas* during his years in Europe—perhaps, his best revenge against his critics.

Morris tells his truths, not only in his works but to the media. His comments on the dance world did not always curry favor, which has resulted in his reputation as an "enfant terrible" or "bad boy of dance." In Joan Acocella's terrific book *Mark Morris,* she mentions a review in 1990 in *The New York Times* that describes his work as camp. "The use of a genuine talent in the service of camp flamboyance . . . is a side of his personality, both offstage and on, that immediately removes him from the artistic lineage so often claimed for him." Accordingto Acocella, that accusation galled him deeply, and the designation of Morris's work as camp probably had as much to do with his public persona as with the work.

When I spoke to Morris about the label of *enfant terrible,* he told me, "That is what other people say about me, and I am for free speech. You can say whatever you think, but I don't have to agree with it. First of all, *enfant terrible* is used without any understanding of what it means. It's text meaning: 'bad boy.' It's so easy to say if you find that someone doesn't live or think the way you do. It's a form of conformism, and I disagree with that on every level. It means that I don't conform to something."

No matter what criticisms may be of Morris, no one can accuse
him of lack of craft or passion about dancemaking. He told one reporter at the *Washington Post,* "I can defend every single measure
of my choreography. I can explain what it means in a court of art."
It is both a revelatory and a powerful quote.

Morris has received his due in recent years. Critics adore him,
and his audiences flock to see his choreographic and operatic pieces,
both in the States and internationally. I wonder if he ever thinks
about the times when he used to scavenge Canal Street in New York
to costume his dancers on the cheap? Now he can afford to work
with the A-list in fashion design with noted people like Isaac
Mizrahi and Donna Karan. The future looks secure for Morris and
his company. Construction began last year in Brooklyn, New York,
for the permanent home for the Mark Morris Dance Group.

IN PRAISE OF MARK MORRIS

THEY LOOK LIKE US

The members of the Mark Morris Dance Group are a melange of
body types, nationalities, and ages. Many of the dancers have been
performing with the company since its inception in 1980. No
sylphs here—the dancers have a healthy physicality bearing little re-
semblance to the anorexic look of dancers in more than a few
dance companies. During my first interview with him, I commented
on that fact and he told me,

> All dancers are real people, even the ones who are encour-
> aged to develop eating disorders; they are still real people.
> But I know what you mean because it's true, and it's not
> what they look like physically. I encourage people not to
> lie. Of course, there is a certain amount of pretend because
> it is the theatre. I can tell if I am watching dancers and they
> are lying. When you see people on stage who are looking at
> each other, and they actually aren't: that doesn't quite
> mean the same thing as actually looking at somebody. It
> can be the exact thing physically, but it is a kinesthetic
> thing that is more interesting and more engaging to me.

The members of the company are technically gifted, but they must have more than superior technical abilities, for Morris's command of the movement lexicon is enormous. His choreography is not made from a single movement vocabulary but from an entire choreographic orchestra. Years of experience and familiarity with his techniques provide a rich background. These dancers know how to dance "from the inside," which is rare; they sing a dance and breathe the movements. They move with internal intelligence, and we easily fall under their spell of gesture.

HIS MOTHER MAXINE

Morris dedicates each of his programs to his mother, Maxine, and God. Mrs. Morris is the type of mother who every artistic child dreams of. It was her love of dance that led her to take the seven-year-old boy to a flamenco concert in their hometown of Seattle, Washington. After that performance, he declared that he would be a flamenco dancer. That almost happened. If he hadn't become disillusioned and disgusted with his experiences studying flamenco in Spain as a young man amidst a harrasing and homophobic climate, perhaps he would have become one of the world's finest. Echoes of his training in and his love for flamenco are evident in some of Morris's work.

Morris's family originates from a "let's pretend" sensibility in all it's glory. Making art in various forms was simply part and parcel of his wonderbread years, and his house was alive with creative projects: a film, a play, or a musical venture. His grandfather had a penchant for presenting performances in their home and dressing up in costumes. Morris's uncle used to make home movies starring none other than Morris and his sister. It was a fertile background for any budding genius. While other children were reading *Mad* magazines and shooting off firecrackers, Morris was studying at the Verla Flowers Dance Studio, and when he wasn't dancing, he was reading the encyclopedia.

HIS TEACHER, VERLA FLOWERS

Verla Flowers is well educated about various forms of dance, and it was soon obvious to her that the young Morris boy was a unique student. She broke the rules when she accompanied the eleven-year-old to an audition to study with the legendary dancer José Greco. She persuaded Greco to let him audition, even though he was much younger than the other dancers at the tryouts. Greco was so impressed with his dancing that he told her that Morris's dancing reminded him "of himself at that age." He won the scholarship, and in a local newspaper article, Mrs. Morris told the reporter, "I think he was dancing before he was walking. He was born doing it."

In the late 1960s, Morris danced in a variety of recitals at Flowers's studio. He tap-danced a number with a group called "Frenchy Brown," and in 1971, he choreographed his first ballet called *Boxcar Boogie* and other works followed. Morris was so knowledgeable that Flowers often let the young boy teach classes, easily recognizing and nurturing his talents. Her willingness to allow Morris to choreograph, teach, and explore different forms of dance were an important contribution to his later versatility. She provided him with a rich training ground that would serve him well.

HIS MUSICALITY

The virtues of a Mark Morris work lie in the musicality of the piece.

In a cookie-cutter world of choreography, he has a cleverness of phrasing that is rare, akin to jazz stylist Johnny Hartman's unique sound: pure, rich, and without artifice. Morris, like Hartman, not only respects the music but fully resides in it. Hartman's voice is truth, and so are Morris's dancers. They don't move outside or inside the music, only in it. Morris's insight and comprehensive understanding of music is daunting, and he frequently studies the compositions he chooses for great lengths of time, to know every chord, every change, every note, before he sets the work.

HIS VERSATILITY

What gives me pause is not only the breadth of a Morris work but the range of the work: sacred pieces, *Stabat Mater,* the humorous *The Hard Nut, Behemoth* (the only piece he made without music), *Three Preludes,* and the black-humoured piece about vampires, *One Charming Night.*

I met with Morris on two occasions. Before the first meeting, I was told to expect an outrageous interview and that Morris was often "over-the-top." I was enchanted by our conversation and found him utterly facinating with a very quick mind and an engaging sense of humor. During our second meeting held at a small hotel in San Francisco, a pianist played in the background while we spoke. At one point in the conversation, Morris leapt to his feet to correct the tempo of the pianist's rendition of the music he was playing.

Morris was quite generous with his time and opinions. When I walked to my car after the interview, I kept thinking that wouldn't it be great if I could arrange a panel discussion with Morris, Noel Coward, Mozart, George Balanchine, and Martha Graham?

I am struck by your ability to blend the sacredness of dance with humor, which is rare. Can you tell me more about your creative process?

I am loathe to use the term *creative process* because people have made that magic, and it's not; it's work. I refer to it as making up a dance because that is what I do. I do a lot of question-and-answer sessions after a performance, and people will ask me, "When you listen to the music and visualize the dance . . . ," I say, "Stop, wait, wait, wait." Maybe that is what *you* do, but when I listen to music, I don't visualize the dance. I just listen to the music, and then if I decide to make up a dance to something, I make it up. It doesn't occur to me in a vision.

I do a lot of preparatory work musically, and I listen to the music because I love the music, and there are more years of it and more kinds of it and higher standards than there are for dance. Music is generally of a higher quality. You can get away with anything in a dance show, *anything*. Any creative artist chooses whatever creative rules he or she is interested in that they want to put forth in a particular work of art. Very often dancing to me should be better than it is: choreography and dancing and the music that goes with it.

How does the dance get created? Do you work out the choreography when you listen to the music?

I choose music that I love that I can stand to listen to many, many times. I study the score and I do all of the preparatory work in my room, analyzing the score. Generally that generates some ideas for tone or situation or the kind of action that should happen. I don't really make up the choreography until I am in the room with the dancers, because I like to do that better.

When I watch your work, there is a purity about it. The bodies of the dancers don't lie; the movements don't lie; it's very clean. What's the process like for you when you are creating a work?

The first thing I do, is that I have no ideas. I announce to everyone, "I have no idea what I am going to do." It's not true, and I am usually lying. But I have no ideas, and then I make up something, and then I make up something else, and it's too complicated, and I simplify it, and I use those ideas to make a whole dance. At a certain point I usually don't allow new material because I have decided on the language of a particular dance, and that's it! It's a closed system. This will happen for that twenty-two minutes in this language.

So you are saying that once the ideas are there, there are certain parameters and a certain language that will be given to that particular dance.

Yes. I was reading Haydn doing that in the *Symphonies,* and it's not unusual. I'm not comparing myself with Haydn, but it's not unusual with just about every artist I know. Some people work on a painting for ten years and the viewer will say, "My five-year-old could have done that in five minutes." It's true and it's not true. This is simple. In *Orpheus and Eurydice,* I said, "here's the material I have to work with." That included a great deal of study, and the reading of Virgil and Ovid and the classical sources, and the music and the libretto and other treatments of Monteverdi and Glück, and reading about how Orpheus is treated. Then I decided that I had enough information and vowed that I wanted it to be simple and direct. And that's very hard.

It's very hard to make things simple as an artist.

Yes. It's much easier to make something very complicated and dazzling than it is to make up something that is smaller and direct. That's why I think every artist I know, especially ones who have been around a few years, does that. In Haydn, with his symphonies, it's easier to write yourself out of a corner by adding special effects, but it has to be built up within the piece and be answered in its own language. You can't suddenly introduce something from another lexicon to solve a problem in dance. You can as a special effect, as a little twist, but it's the easier way. It has to be constructed strongly enough that it can't be knocked over, and that was Haydn's problem and everyone's problem as an artist.

It's so hard as a writer to write simply and clearly. It's damn difficult.

Of course it is. It's easy to make fun of Hemingway because he's so butch and so terse and so spare. He also says a great deal—I think he is good. Or Satie, people who do these things that are obviously simplified or pared down, like John Cage or Bach. Nowadays, it's hard to recognize that which has been simplified. It seems as if it is exaggerated, but it's not. It's very, very clear. There isn't a wasted breath in it.

Do you create a work to please yourself first? Do you think of the audience?

Sure, we are performing artists, so of course it is for other people to watch. But, if I don't base it on what pleases me or satisfies me structurally and entertainment-wise . . . the fact is, I have a certain instinct and a certain skill and certain feeling that enough people recog-

nize or empathize with, and that is why the work is popular. I don't
think, "This will knock them dead." I think, "This will knock me dead,
and I hope other people enjoy watching it." I have a lot of experience
watching dance and many other art forms and participating in them so
I know. I don't work in a vacuum. It's not Broadway, which *is* a vacuum.

Do you often use visual sources? Is that helpful to you?

Sure, but it's also from a lifetime of looking at pictures and build-
ings and people and music. It's my life. It's something I know. I can
say, "Oh, wait, that reminds me of painting by Schoenberg that I think
is beautiful." Or, I may see what *Bullfinch's Mythology* has to say
about this, and choose to use it or not. When I did my research for
Orpheus and Eurydice I was also looking at Greco-Roman antiquities
because I wanted it to be more Hellenistic than it was. It looked too
. . . something, and I wanted it to look like something else. Part of it
is an assignment. When I was working on a Monteverdi piece, I was
listening to Cavalli. I will listen to Cavalli and Monteverdi and other
pieces because I learn more about Monteverdi, and I know a lot
about Monteverdi, but I want to know *more.* Then I will go through a
translation with a friend of mine who is Italian and get the words
specifically that I don't understand in Italian. I just want to know
more. It's not like, "Now, Mark, you are making up a dance like this
so you must check it out in the library." It's not fuel, but it's substance; it's information. Information is interesting to me.

What do you read?

Everything. I read lots and lots of different things. I read poetry a
lot. I am reading now *The Memoirs of Hadrian* by Marguerite Ysource-
nar. It's a great, great book. I just reread *The Metamorphosis of Ovid*
recently because it's great. I am also reading a translation that someone sent me of *Beauty and the Beast.* It's a beautiful story. I also
read magazines and novels.

Are you familiar with Jeanette Winterson's book *Art Objects?*
It's a wonderful book. I think you would appreciate it.

No, I don't know it. One of the greatest books on art that I have ever read is *The Story of Art* by E. L. Gombrich, which was written in the 40s or 50s. It's one of the most fabulous, eloquent, and beautiful books of art history that I have ever read. You may think, "What am I, in junior high? I don't need to read this." But then you read it, and it's a beautiful, beautiful book. There is another book that I read sometimes. It's by the same guy, and it's called *The Sense of Order.* It's about ornamentation and design, and it covers needlepoint and calligraphy, and the compulsion to fill things and how that is done. He talks about the fundamentals of symmetry and design. He covers William Morris wallpaper and Islamic ceramics and everything in-between, and what's called crafts. He's a genius. It's been very informative to me, and it relates to music in a beautiful way.

Speaking of form, would you say that your choreography has a Duncan influence in it at all?

I think it is the same effect that Blake has on my work. Who has ever seen a Duncan work? I have seen beautiful reconstructions. I have seen the same photographs and the same ten seconds of newsreel that everyone else has. But the fact is that aside from coming from the Orientalist school and the Denishawn school with barefoot dancing, esthetic dancing from the turn of the century was inseparable from feminism. They were the same thing. It was like in *The Music Man,* the Grecian-urn number when Hermione Gingold does barefoot dancing. It's very funny, but it's a comment on that period of early feminism and mysticism and taking off your corset and shoes. That was the biggest thing about it. It wasn't about "I danced like her." This was the first time that Americans just danced around, and why is this less valid than something else? That's the important part.

In the States, she was treated poorly, shunned, and received terrible reviews.

She was just too much. She was a big woman who was barefoot and danced without a girdle and underpants. She was a radical feminist, and that's interesting.

You wanted to be a flamenco dancer at an early age and studied in Spain. Has that study influenced your work?

I don't use direct quotations. My experience is with Spanish dance and Balkan dance forms, a bunch of national dance forms. It has to do with a certain way, a preference of ways to move, and how to relate to music and rhythm and vocal music. You sing and dance with other people, so it's not so much presentational as it is participatory. Flamenco itself among many Spanish dance forms is basically a solo form. It's a form of informed improvisation, the way Indian dance or Indian music and certain jazz forms function. Bel canto, singing in Baroque music, is also the same sort of thing where you are ornamenting something and it's real and fundamental. That is very interesting. The comportment of my dancers in my choreography is different from other people's work because of everything I have been through, including Spanish dance and different national dance forms. Everything I have ever done is fuel.

I am stuck by your use of the body in your works, and the fact that your dancers are not anorexic-looking. They look like "real people."

All dancers are real people, even the ones who are encouraged to develop eating disorders. They are still real people. But I know what you mean, because it is true, and it's not just what they look like physically. I encourage people not to lie. Of course, there is a certain amount of pretend because this is the theatre.

What do you mean by "lying"?

I can tell if I am watching dancers who are lying. When you see people on stage who are looking at each other but they actually aren't, they are looking in the direction of one another as if they are saying, "Now, we turn our heads towards each other," that doesn't quite mean the same thing as actually looking at somebody. It can be the same thing physically, but it is a kinesthetic thing that is more interesting and more engaging to me.

Because the movement is "true," the movement is authentic?

Yes. They are right next to you: "Oh, hello, I know you." That's interesting to me and that's a real person thing. It's not just the fact that there are breasts and buttocks and racial variety.

Your dances are very compelling. They have a Jungian perspective with a utopian vision and its dark side. That contrast is stimulating to watch. You often see those elements in opera frequently, but not so much in dance.

You should. If it's done well, it exists in every good piece of art. There isn't one thing by itself. It's always contexual, always. It can't *not* be. It's life. You can't just have prettiness. Some people go to the ballet because it's pretty, and that's sad because the ballet is just pretty. It shouldn't even exist because it should be in relation to something else. Why is that beautiful and this is not? Beauty doesn't exist separately. It exists in the world of everything else and it is also subjective, which is why you can't please all the people all the time, nor would you want to.

Would you say that any of your works are autobiographical?

Yes. I would. There is a piece called *The Vacant Chair,* a piece called *Jealousy,* and there are certain aspects of *The Hard Nut,* at least in the first act, that are drawn from autobiographical incidents and characters, sort of. It's not my life, but it's based on people I knew, so it's autobiographical a little bit. You don't have to be happy to make up a happy dance. It's theatre; it's a fantasy. You don't have to be unhappy to make up an unhappy dance, and anything in between. It's part of your job to mine your ideas and your emotions and your feelings, and you decide how to deal with it. If an opera singer stirs you to tears, it's because of her artistry, not because she herself is crying, and you are crying in sympathy. You are crying in identification of what she is presenting as an artist, and that's where people go wrong a lot.

Do you mean in understanding dance performance?

Where, I think, dance fails very often is where people are trying to make something happen to me as a viewer, instead of allowing it to happen.

You mean you are manipulated into feeling a certain way?

Mark Morris Dance Group in *L'Allegro, il Penseroso ed il Moderato.*
Copyright Gadi Dagon. Courtesy of the Mark Morris Dance Group.

Of course, it's manipulative because it's an artifice of theatre, but it can be manipulative and smart or manipulative and cheap. "Manipulative" isn't necessarily derogatory. But you want to involve people and you want to engage people, and there is a chance of communicating something. I don't know what "that" is, but just to open that channel is an important thing in art of any kind, not just in choreography.

What do you think about using the personal in one's work?

You can't not. There is no way not to. How can you as a human being not be influenced by your life as a human being? People imagine that there is a "leave it at the door" idea, which I agree with. There is professional conduct and responsibility, but there is fantastic nourishment from who you are and how you feel as an artist.

Have you made any pieces from the past that now you would change?

Sure. If I bring back an old dance, I don't change it *ever.* Why? Why should I? If the dance is from 1981, that is what I did then, and I want to be as faithful to that as I can. Otherwise, if you adjust everything, you will end up making one piece, and it's always exactly the same idea because you are revising.

I didn't see *Behemoth,* but it interested me a great deal. It is intriguing to me for someone like you who has a heightened sense of musicality to choose not to use music.

The piece is still musical, it's just unaccompanied. It's built according to musical principles, but you aren't listening to anything at the same time. That's another case when I came into the studio and said, "I have no idea what to do." Usually, I can stand with a score and pretend that I am thinking of something, instead of just standing there. After a couple of weeks, I had an hour or more of material.

Did you know when you went into the studio that you wouldn't choose to use musical accompaniment?

Yes. That was my mission in that dance since I use music all the time, and I wondered what would happen if I didn't use music. It didn't make me want to do that all the time. But there are parts in my dances where I work in stretches that I just want to have happen where it's not rhythmicized. There's a duration, and it takes a certain amount of time, but it's not divided by beat. I do that all the time. When you see and hear something that is organized by music, it is rhythmicizing itself, you hear and watch it at the same time. Whether it's beat for beat or not, or big washes of things, it still looks like it has a relationship to the music because it happens at the same time.

I want to talk about your use of space, the symmetry of it, the beauty of the line, even though the movements may not be a "beautiful shape." When you are working, are you thinking about the audience's perception at all?

Sure. I rehearse from the front of the studio. Absolutely. I make it up to be "watched." It's not enough just "to do." That's contact improvisation. Of course, I love the proscenium. I had an experiment with myself, and I am still doing it, where I decided to banish diagonals from my work. Years ago, I made up a dance that was only set on the modern dance diagonal, "that thing" that is always in modern dance. First I did only a modern dance diagonal dance in order to purge myself of that. Then I spent a long time making up dances that had no diagonals traveling in them, because, in the classroom, that's the longest trip across the floor from point to point. It's longer than either of the sides in the studio by several feet. Also, because of the tradition of classical ballet (which I love, the way it's staged), because everything is focused in the front and you do everything downhill, it augments jumps and it makes jumps look higher.

In classical ballet of the nineteenth century, and when you go into Balanchine's work, you do a diagonal, and you run into the next corner and do another diagonal thing, and that's because you can show what people look like from all angles from the front. You don't just want to see people straight on, I think. People don't want to see that.

Why not?

Well, it's not because it was abolished. People stopped doing that because they wanted to see 3-D all the time. On purpose, I stopped doing that. I did circles and I was working with poles. I was working with up and down, and right and left, and doing as little as I could on the diagonal. It doesn't mean that it doesn't exist, it means I am very conscious of when I use that because it's an automatic thing that dancers and choreographers do. People don't move straight-side very well; you have to be going forward. People don't move backwards well or sideward well; they move forward well because of how we are built. But I decided that I didn't want that anymore, so I stopped doing it.

Would you enact certain parameters that you want to work with just for the challenge?

Yes. Also it develops a product that you couldn't have predicted completely. There is a piece called *Beautiful Day* that I made that modern dancers love, and students love it because it is very swirly-looking. It's a duet. My problem with it is that I decided not to use any curves or spirals in the piece, so it's angles only, because there are two dancers leaning on each other and the force of the pulling makes it spiral-looking by the way in which it is built. The way it is put together with counter balances makes it looks swirly. But it's actually not.

So, the design fulfilled its purpose.

Yes. It made a beautiful spiral that you can't do by saying, "And now, spiral." You can only do it by saying, "Don't ever spiral." The physics of the dance make it spiral.

That would make it a lot more interesting for you.

Sure, and for everybody involved.

I want to talk about the religious themes in *Gloria* and *Stabat Mater*. Can you talk about those works?

Stabat Mater is a very interesting piece. *Gloria* is a smash hit, and I have been doing it for many years. *Stabat* is a thornier piece, no pun intended, and it's one that I adore, and I think is beautiful and fabulous.

What was the inspiration for those pieces?

The music and the text. That's all. You know, much of the greatest art of the world was inspired by religious affiliation, if not feeling. It was unheard of to be a nonreligious person, not that long ago; you just were. There was no option.

Are you talking about fifty years ago?

No, more than that, 150 years ago. In the eighteenth century, you were Catholic or Protestant (if we are talking about Western Europe now) or a heretic, which you couldn't choose, of course. The households sponsored works of music at the churches that had a Kappellmeister, who needed new music for the Mass every Sunday. That was a great commissioned gig for a composer. That's fine with me. How does a Bach cantata deny women the right to be priests? It doesn't. How do Bach's church cantatas condemn homosexuality? They don't. The church does that. Music doesn't do that. It's impossible for music to do that.

Music doesn't speak to just one segment of society.

Well, that is debatable, because it can speak to a particular culture and that's fine; I have no problem with that. I have no problem
with Western European music; I don't feel guilty about it. I love South-
east Asian music, I love West African music, and I also, frankly, like
those things because they are foreign to me, and through that, they
give me access.

What do you like about music that isn't familiar to you?

I love South Indian music partly because it's not like the music
that I grew up with. It's not just as orientalia, as exotica; it's a legitimate, fabulous form of music that is from serious thought. Much Indian music is also from a religious character. It's not Lutheran, but
it's communicative and evocative of a particular spiritual aspect.
Much music is like that even if it's not affiliated with religion.

It's sacred music and it was used specifically for that purpose.

That's something that made great music happen. I am an atheist,
but I don't deny anyone's right to believe in anything if it produces a
fabulously beautiful, moving product. Everyone is better for that.

**I know you have a roomful of religious icons. I am a Marian fa-
natic. Can you tell me about the room?**

I am a Marian too. It's not just Jesus icons; its Mary and many of
the saints. I like how those things look and what they mean to people. Someone came to visit and saw my room and, missing the point
totally, they said, "Do you collect kitsch and religious articles?" What
is the difference? How is a pink, plastic crucifix different from a fif-
teenth-century Armenian icon that is a sacred relic? It's not different;
there is no difference at all. It means the same thing.

Are you religious at all, Mark?

I am basically an atheist, but I am very, very interested in matters
religious and spiritual. What better music was produced than Bach's
writing on religious themes? There isn't anything. There is nothing
better. This started when I was more of a pantheist. I am not anymore. I am an atheist, but that doesn't mean that I don't think about

these things. It means that they are very, very interesting to me.

I would like to know your feelings about this: Do you believe that dancers are privy to a particular consciousness, a sacred energy when they dance? I mean that those feelings are articulated through the body without intellectual thought.

No, I don't think that. I think that the way one works in order to be a dancer, working with the body all the time, working with other people all the time, working with the music, working in a strange state—it's a strange thing. By working that way, you are exposed more frequently to things that are not able to be defined, not able to be verbalized, but that isn't necessarily spiritualism or subconscious or the universal something. I would take that and go to atoms and molecules, and I would go into biology and physics with that. It's the same route; it's the same as Big Bang theory; it's the same as Bach; it's the same as a lot of things.

Have you ever experienced when dancing a more heightened or trancelike state?

Is heightened the same as trancelike? No, it is not.

It's levels of experience and one's individual perception of that experience.

But again, that is biological to me. If we are talking about different waves reproduced or different states of repose or breathing in patterns, sure, that happens, but also running in a marathon makes you feel a certain way. Sleep deprivation makes you feel a certain way. Religious ecstasy makes you feel a certain way. Mescaline makes you feel a certain way. Everything makes you feel different, and that is great. But when one is performing, and one is good, and one is confident, and one is skilled, then one is capable of existing in what is often called "flow state," when you are working and everything seems to be great, it seems to be that automatic writing kind of thing. That can be worshipped and thereby trivialized, or it can just be part of what you do. When you are performing in front of many people with live music, you don't necessarily think, "Right, left, right." You can also just do what you are doing. I don't know if that is height-ened. What's the opposite of heightened? It is lowered. It's less. It's not a heightened awareness. It's exclusive awareness. It's being aware of fewer things, not more things. It's how these things match up without words. If that's heightened, then yes. If that's some sort of spiritual something, then sure. It is semantics.

I wondered what that would feel like in the body.

It depends on the person. I don't know how any other person feels.

I am addressing this question to you, I want to know how you feel.

I am most happy when I perform or choreograph when there is ba-sically no difference between stepping off the stage or onstage. I am the same person. I am relaxed and capable and can solve anything any second. I am capable of doing anything I want, and I choose to do this—that's what I want to do. I can't quite do that if I am worried that this might hurt—or I will be late, or my shoes are untied, or how do I deal with that? That is also interesting because it's part of being where you are at the exact moment—"Oh, and my shoes are un-tied"—and you build that in. It's not magic, but it's fabulous and fun and it's probably addictive.

Are you one who engages in rituals?

Yes. I am in the theatre. Maybe you are talking about something else than I am. I am saying that theatre is ritual, performing is a rit-ual, not like the hug circle before the show, or the mayor's gift, or the bouquet of flowers. That is superstition, not ritual. The theatre is one of the oldest rituals on earth; it's bonfire mentality; it's telling a story to somebody. You are in the dark watching and we are conveying something to you—that's the ritual; that's it.

I am curious to know if you have a specific ritual that you do, or did, before you perform or watch your work? I know some perform-ers do.

No. I warm up, I put on my makeup. I am not superstitious and I am not nostalgic. I think people get tricked by those feelings, by sentimentality or by anxiety. I think it is very often anxiety. What is often called clairvoyance is often just anxiety.

You are always involved in so many projects. Do you ever have any spare time in your schedule? What do you like to do with that time?

I listen to music and read and have dinner. There is not a bit of difference between my work and my life. I can't leave my work at the office. I *am* my office. Sometimes I listen to music to purge the music that is stuck in my head. I have many things that overlap that are fascinating to me. I only do what I want, and there aren't a lot of people who only do what they want. I guess there are a few serial killers.

It's a gift to only do the work you want.

It's a gift and it's a decision. It's easy for me because my life is heaven, but it is also hell fifty percent of the time.

Why?

What I do is really hard, and I put myself into that situation. It's mostly personal hell, deciding that something is bullshit and I have to put it away or tell someone that they aren't working out. I put off difficult situations as much as I can, like most people. It's the hell of resolving the last few minutes of a piece to make it work without introducing new material. I forget that the easy part was a few weeks ago when I was making up things freely. Now I have to rectify it and the system has to close, and that is hard. It's my own fault. It's fun and it's also hell.

When you go to sleep, are you thinking of these things? Are you able to shut it off? You have such a quick mind.

That depends. I had a few days off in Seattle, and when I was trying to go to sleep, every moment I was hearing music from *Orpheo,* and I wasn't even working on it. I was finished with that. I would wake up and read to change my attention. I like to sleep about nine or ten hours.

I am a big fan of sleeping.

It's wonderful, it's underrated.

Do you keep track of your dreams?

I know them. Since I have a company, I can tell everyone about a dream I just had, and there are twenty people waiting around who I am paying. If they started that, I would tell them to shut up and get to work. We talk about things all the time. We love dreams.

Do you use any of the ideas you may get in dreams?

How can a dream not be helpful?

Some people don't pay attention.

I do. But I don't have a dream guide. Problems aren't solved in dreams. They are a reflection of what happened before. Very often they do not necessarily guide you to what's going on. They are often very tonally interesting.

I like to pay attention since I find my dreams very helpful.

In my mother's dreams, she flies and she dances. In mine, I nearly never fly or dance. I converse or have sex or walk around in mine.

Tell me a little more about your mother. She has been a terrific influence in your life and I have enjoyed my conversations with her.

What do you want to know?

What do you want to tell me?

She reminds me of two other darling friends near her age: Merce Cunningham and Lou Harrison. Those two gentlemen remind me of my mother because they are around the same age, they are all Westerners, they are a certain generation, they have a certain droll and are very polite, very strong, very opinionated, and so kind and impatient. Those three people, those two old guys and my mom remind me of one another a great deal. Lou Harrison is not the friend I have had the longest, but he is my friend who is the oldest, and that's interesting to me. It's not even a mentor thing. I think that Lou is great. My mother reminds me of this. She is great all the time.

What is the best advice you ever received?

Mark Morris and his mother. *Reproduced by permission of Maxine Morris.*

One piece of advice I got twenty years ago was from choreographer Lar Lubovitch, who said to me, "You aren't going to start a company, are you?" It wasn't my intention, but then I did. I don't know if this was advice or a warning. Now, in the present, if I am having a difficult rehearsal, I will say to someone, "I hope you start a dance company. May you start a dance company of your own someday." Like a curse. "Then you will understand." That was what he was saying and it's true. That was good advice. And the things you hear about what people say about you are always interesting.

Can you give me an example?

Some guy I never liked, who I knew ten years earlier, ended up as a producer and he was bringing us to town. I heard him describe me as "an old, drunk, fat queen" or something like that. And I said, "Ok, I am old. I drink. I am fat. OK, you are right." How can that be insulting? It was like, "Fuck you and here is my beautiful show."

What would you say is one of the greatest misconceptions about the dance world?

I can't talk about the whole dance world.

***Your* dance world, Mark.**

That it's an accident. There are a lot of critics who say, "He obviously didn't have the capacity to work in this form." Or they say, "Everything was fabulous except the costumes." If you don't like the ending, sorry. I tried the one you wanted and it was stupid. You will just have to live with it. If you didn't like it, that's fine, but you can't wish it was something else. Or they say that I didn't have enough ideas to do this the way they wish it would turn out. Guess what? I had the ideas I had and here is my dance. That's it. It's just a dance.

Does it bother you when critics don't get it?

I don't know what it is to get. I don't describe my work, and I won't. I will to the people involved; I will use images or descriptions. It's the thinking that "I couldn't think of something," or "It was an accident." It was not. I decided that; I chose that person to do that part.

It has nothing to do with like or dislike. It doesn't have to do with esthetics, it has to do with ignorance. I never promised you would like it. I promised that I will present it as well as I can.

Does it bother you if the critic doesn't like it?

I don't care as long as it's well written and well argued.

Do you read what people write about you?

Yes. I read everything. I am very tired at very lazy journalism. There's a lot of that, where people just write about things they read that somebody else wrote. "Oh, I hear Mark Morris is like this. . . ." And that becomes fact. It's not. It is just someone's opinion. It's all third-generation fantasy and that's fine. People are shocked that I am actually articulate and relatively intelligent and not evil.

Evil? What do you mean?

They say, "Watch out, I have heard he is like this." Let's make some people question, and if they take pause, then it is fine; then I can do what I do without interruption. It's fine if people ask the same questions and I give a similar answer. But if someone's research is just reading other articles about me, it's not necessarily true just because it appears in a publication. But scandal makes better copy.

You said in an interview (correct me if I am wrong), that some of your work makes people uncomfortable. What did you mean?

Well, sure, it's true. I know that because I have been performing for many years and some people are uncomfortable with some of my work, and that's fine. It's not necessarily the point, but I can't represent every single person's taste. If you did that, you would have Disneyland—totally homogenized. That is not interesting to me artistically, let alone personally.

When you see a performance that is flawed, does that affect you? Are you a perfectionist about your work in some manner?

Yes. In some manner, but that is not always in agreement with what other people think is a perfect situation. In coaching dance, I say that it is more important to get the dynamics right, the kinetics right, the action right, the phrasing right, and the tone right than it is to be exactly on the quarter mark or to be exactly in line with somebody: it's easy to be in line with somebody: It's easy to be in the right place on the stage. It's much harder to reimagine what you are doing on the stage every time so it is real, it's not by rote, it is not just a bunch of moves. Everyone thinks and feels and learns differently, and although I want a certain amount of precision, that is not the only goal. There are more important attributes to dancers then obedience; there is imagination and intelligence. You don't have to be smart to be obedient. You have to be smart to be a good artist.

A dancer can be technically proficient, yet dancing with passion from the "inside" is something else. Can you teach that type of internal dancing?

You can encourage it, or adjust it, or promote it. There are people who have fabulous passion and artistic intelligence who are terrible technicians. I don't want to see them either.

Has there ever been a time in your life when you doubted your own abilities?

Daily. Well, sure. I am not paralyzed with grief or self-doubt, but I think, "How can I pull this one off?" When is everyone going to realize that I'm a charlatan?" Or, they did already, and I'm not. Who says it goes like this instead of like this? It's my decision and I am fully responsible for it. It's not a divine gift. Fifteen years ago I had a crisis. I also had a crazy boyfriend who was also an artist and who imagined that I should stop choreographing and be a waiter. Well, every dancer is a waiter, but I never was. I never did anything but dance *ever* in my life. I never had any other job. Why do I have to be more like you? Can't I be more like me? That's one problem I have with people who want you to be more like they are. I have a bit of a problem with that. That is the definition of conservatism.

Well, it is reassuring to them, and validates their own choices.

Right. Well, I dumped the bastard. But I really doubted because I thought I was doing a worthless job and I wasn't making a contribution to society. The fact is, I am making a giant contribution to society through art. It doesn't mean I am a genius or fabulously gifted. I am a good choreographer, I know that. I am not finding a cure for AIDS. It's not science but it's solace, and beauty is enough.

Beauty is far more than enough. Mark, can you address the gifts of fame? What has fame given to you?

It means that I can get a table in a restaurant that's booked up. It's true, and that's nothing to sneeze at.

Especially in New York.

Exactly. I get free tickets to things all the time: fashion shows, openings, and parties. I have access to things that I wouldn't otherwise, and I love that. That's fine with me.

Is there a downside of fame?

I get clogged up a lot of the time. I am too busy a lot of the time, but it's my own darn fault.

What about your privacy?

I spend more time alone than I used to. I am more famous and I travel more and in big groups more, but I am also alone more. I am older now, so I like that. I used to feel like I was missing something, and I don't anymore. That's a good thing.

Has being famous hurt you in the sense that you can't do the things you want to do?

It's hard to get a date. Men look at me and I don't know what the look is. I don't know if it's a look that says, "I saw you in *Vogue* magazine," or "I saw you in the movie *Unzipped*," or "I think you are cute and I want to have a date with you," or "I want to dance in your company because I am a really good dancer." I don't know what people want, because they look at me a lot because of who I am. People look at me and it's hard to tell between curiosity and cruising. So it's hard to get a date, but I also want dates less than I used to.

What do you think about the future of dance?

I had a prediction that started out as a joke a few years ago, but now I think it is true. I predicted that at the turn of the century, mime will come back. Mime will come back as a reaction to increased technology. Mime, the simplest sort of street theatre will come back. I don't care about it and I am not promoting it. Opera is big and will be; modern dance might disappear, and classical ballet is waning.

Why do you think that modern dance may disappear?

My feeling is that there is a possibility that American modern dance is a movement like the Soviet Union, which lasted about seventy or seventy-five years, and there is a chance that modern dance as a subset of dance in general could diminish to nothing in a couple of decades.

Do you think that the dance will fade because of problems with lack of funding and problems with NEA?

No, no, no. The NEA is irrelevant. I mean as an art form. Art forms don't depend on sponsorship. I am not denying sponsorship; I think it is the most important thing in the world. That's the difference between the American and the European system. Art is a necessity in Europe and a luxury in the United States because of some sort of fake frontier nostalgia that people have, this sort of Norman Rockwell, bootstrap mentality that is represented and has increased worldwide in fundamentalism of every stripe. Modern dance is a special interest, and maybe it's just time for it to go away. It's possible. Elizabethan verse drama lasted a certain time and went away, like Impressionism, like any sort of ism—modern dance-ism. We will see. I don't want it to go away, because it's my only skill.

4

Catherine Turocy

"Her choreographic needle is sharp but flexible and its embroidery is densely vivid."

———Molly McQuade, Dance Magazine

Catherine Turocy in costume. *Copyright 1991 by Lois Greenfield.*

Catherine Turocy, artistic director and cofounder of the New York
Baroque Dance Company for over two decades, has not only taken
on the duties of "les filles de Mémoire" of this noble art form, but
she is certainly Baroque dance's most accomplished daughter of
memory. Artfully creating and recreating Baroque works with
painstaking accuracy, Turocy's choreography summons us to another time and age when manners, courtly charms, and grandeur
were the order of the day. Her ballets transport audiences into a
vast world of beauty, a world filled with characters from the French
court, women who yearn for their beloveds, men who compete for
their *object d'affection,* and gods and goddesses who frolic and
fancy with the foibles of mortal behavior.

For anyone who admires and appreciates beauty in all of its
forms, Baroque ballet offers satisfaction of the senses and comfort
of the symbolic imagination. The choreographic alphabet of
Baroque gesture and geometry speak through Turocy to communicate all of the intricacies and delicacies of the period, and invokes
the living shadows of historical reference. All of the gestures, costumes, and philosophy of the works are substantive and have their
own language. This organization of gesture, floor patterns, and
music speaks to us if we pay attention to it's unique calligraphy.

She explained further:

> Art in the eighteenth century has always been symbolic. It
> has always meant something. For example, any gesture that
> is up often refers to the heavens or blessings or happiness.
> Any gesture that is down has to do with Mother Earth, or
> with Hades or the devil or a sense of loss. When one ex-
> pands those directions to the body moving in space, one has
> an expressive structure within which to work. The choreog-
> rapher can use these structures to solve choreographic puz-
> zles. Looking at the performing conventions of that day, one
> can see how they relate to today's dance forms.

Baroque ballet is much more subtle than classical ballet, yet this
subtlety does not usurp its power on the stage. Jean Georges
Noverre, a great choreographer of his time, shattered the traditional
view of ballet as "pretty steps" and wrote copiously, insisting that

the ballet should represent action, character, and feeling. In *Two Letters on Dancing,* published in 1760, he proclaimed that

> Dancing is possessed of all of the advantages of a beautiful language, yet it is not sufficient to know the alphabet alone. But when a man of genius arranges the letters from words and connects the words to form sentences, it will cease to be dumb; it will speak with both strength and energy; and then ballets will share with the best plays the merit of affecting and moving, and of making tears flow, and, in their less serious styles, of being able to amuse, captivate, and please. And dancing, embellished with feeling and guided by talent, will at last receive that praise and appaluse which all Europe accords to poetry and painting.

His advice to budding choreographers of his time are apt words for any artist creating today:

> Acquire all the knowledge you can of the matter you have in hand. Your imagination, filled with the pictures you wish to represent, will provide you with the proper figures, steps, and gestures. Then your compositions will glow with fire and strength; they cannot but be true to nature if you are full of your subject. Bring love as well as enthusiasm to your art. To be successful in theatrical representations, the heart must be touched, the soul moved, and the imagination inflamed.

Turocy's historical representations of Baroque dance derive from that sensibility. She even resembles a dancer from another time; she has a regal demeanor, soulful and beguiling eyes, long flowing hair, and a lovely laugh. When she is performing she is able to become her characters, and during our interview she spoke in depth about that transformation. When I asked her about her deep resonance with her work she explained, "I definitely feel an affinity with the century. I don't know if it's from living before or that these elements exist in the universe, but somehow that aesthetic makes sense to me."

Turocy does much more than recreate dances from the past. The reconstruction of this art requires far more than technical virtuosity and the ability to read notation. She delves into the historical documentation of the dance and is able to feel, to intuit, to make real all of the components of the works. Seemingly able to directly communicate with her counterparts of history, she brings back that knowledge and adds it to her artistic process in order to make her own choreographic comments.

Turocy is many things: artist, dancer, scholar, stage director, reconstructor, and dramatist, and her contributions have kept these ballets flourishing. She is careful to include all aspects of the dance performance: music, movement, stage design, costuming, and the philosophical implications of the work.

She was recognized for her artistic achievements in 1995 by the French Ministry of Culture, which awarded her the prestigious rank of Chevaliér for educating audiences around the world on how to understand Baroque dance and how to receive it.

Turocy and her company have performed at Lincoln Center's Mostly Mozart Festival, the Spoleto Festival USA, and in major cities in the world. She has received commissions to choreograph over twenty opera productions, including Rameau's *Les Boréades*, *Les Fêtes d'Hébé*, *Pygmalion*, Handel's *Terpischore*, LeClair's *Scyllet Glaucus*, Charpentier's *Les Arts Florissants*, Purcell's *Dido and Aeneas*, and Mozart's *Le Nozze di Figaro*. Turocy has mounted productions of Glück's *Orfeo* in New York City, Handel's *Ariodante* for the Spoleto Festival USA, and *Arianna Frl Goettingen* for the Handel Festival in Germany. She has worked with conductors John Eliot Gardiner, Christopher Harwood, Nicholas McGegan, and her husband, James Richman.

Many of her ballets have been filmed for both American and French television and have been the feature presentation at the Théâtre du Chatelet in Paris, the Opéra de Lyon, the Teatro de San Carlo of Lisbon, and the Mostly Mozart festival at Lincoln Center. She received the Dance Film Association's Award in 1980 for *The Art of Dancing: An Introduction to Baroque Dance*, a video she created and coproduced with Arts Resources in Collaboration.

As a soloist, she has performed with the Concert Royal, The Handel and Haydn Society, the St. Paul Chamber Orchestra, The

Smithsonian Chamber Players, the English Chamber Soloists, the Boston Early Music Festival, the Vancouver Early Music Festival, and the Aston Magna Festival. In 1994, she toured Japan as a Guest Soloist with Conductor Christopher Hogwood and the Academy of Ancient Music.

A frequent lecturer on the Baroque arts, Turocy has addressed the Royal Academies of Dance in London, Stockholm, and Copenhagen; the Festival Estival in Paris; the Society for Early Music in Tokyo; the Smithsonian Institution; the Kennedy Center; the Juilliard School; the Alvin Ailey School; Yale University; and Barnard College. In an effort to train the next generation of dancers and scholars, she teaches Baroque Ballet Workshops in northern California each summer.

She has worked as a consultant with Edward Villella, artistic director for the Miami City Ballet, and with Clark Tippet of American Ballet Theater. The recipient of many awards and choreography fellowships from the National Endowment for the Arts, the U.S.-France Exchange, and the U.S.–United Kingdom Exchange Fellowships, Turocy has also published widely on the subject of Baroque dance, contributing to many publications, including *Les Goûts-réunis, Dance Magazine, Backstage, Arts International, Opera News*, and the *International Encyclopedia of Dance*.

She is married to James Richman, conductor, harpsichordist, and forté pianist. They have two children, Andrew and Edward.

I met with Catherine Turocy to discuss the evolution of her work and to find out in detail how this lost art speaks to the dance world of today. We spoke for hours while sitting on a park bench in a playground. Her young son was lost in his reverie of play, surrounded by the spectacular views of the San Francisco Bay.

How do you think that Baroque dance can make a statement to dancers and choreographers of the present day?

I think works of the earlier choreographers can offer a great deal to modern dance and ballet choreographers. The beautiful geometry of the choreography and the performing conventions of the Baroque period directly relate to today's art forms.

I know that you studied both ballet and modern dance for many years. Was there a particular moment when you knew that Baroque dance was the form in which you belonged?

No. There wasn't that kind of moment; it was more of a conscious decision. When I moved to New York, I was presenting modern dance concerts of my choreography and I was also working in the eighteenth-century vein. In 1978, I thought it would be interesting to put on a modern dance concert with modern dancers using the vocabulary of movement from the eighteenth century, but the concept of style and the music and the way the dance unfolded would be modern.

The concert was held at the Dance Theater Workshop in New York City. I performed the *Passacaille d'Armide,* and when it was finished, I took off my costume and corset on stage, revealing my tie-dyed leotard. I put on a tunic more reminiscent of Isadora Duncan and danced a sarabande in her style. The next kind of dance was a minuet/tango with Charles Garth. Eventually, we got to the later twentieth century, and the last piece I did was to Judy Garland's singing "I Got Rhythm," with twelve dancers dancing with pinwheels à la Busby Berkeley.

People really loved the concert, and they told me it was a lesson for them in dance history. I discovered I had a certain freedom when I wasn't restricting myself to what I thought was the style of the Baroque. I also recognized that I had not fully defined the "style" of Baroque dance in my own work.

Did you feel as though you would have to make a choice between modern dance and the Baroque style?

Yes. I felt that if I were going to continue the research and do original work in the historical dance field, I had to make a decision. I couldn't develop myself both as a modern dance choreographer and a historical choreographer at the same time. I had a talk with a friend, and that conversation brought to mind questions for me about the art of dance and the dance field in general. What kind of work did the field need? Did they need another Twyla Tharp, or did they need somebody who was going to look at Baroque dance from a performer's perspective? I came to the conclusion that I would be serving the dance field in a better way with my talents if I investigated the seventeenth and the eighteenth centuries.

Can you tell me more about the most important influences on your work?

When I was living in New York, I had the opportunity to look at Paul Taylor's work, Balanchine's, Robbins's, and Jirí Kylián's. In any good choreographer's work, any master work, there is something about it that identifies why dance is an art and why it is so important. When you are around great masters like that, you can see their craft and you can study their technique by observing the performances. You don't want to imitate them, but you want to understand what works. I find particularly inspirational the eighteenth-century writings about art and what dance "should be."

How detailed are those readings in terms of descriptions?

The readings often reveal how a performer can make a piece come to life. They are as specific as finding a period description of Marie Sallé's dance, when she brought tears to the spectator's eyes as a dancer in a harem who was not chosen by the sultan to be his concubine for the evening. For example, in the book *A Miscellany for Dancers,* a writer describes Marie Sallé's in performance in *L'Europe Galante:*

> One read in her expression a whole range of emotions; one saw her hesitating between fear and hope; but, at the moment when the Sultan gives the handkerchief to his favorite wife, her whole being quickly underwent a change. She tore herself away from the stage with that degree of despair, characteristic of tender and passionate beings, which is expressed only in utter dejection.

Only Sallé brought those qualities to the stage. When you read a description like that, it does suggest that there had to be high moments of serious drama in dance. That type of dancing is not notated; it reveals itself more in the gestural language of the actor. It's this part that inspires me. I read those descriptions and try to recreate that in my own dancing. I find that a challenge.

I remember reading about Mr. Balanchine when he was working with Diaghilev at the Ballet Russes. He was told to study the paintings and the sculpture of the times. I always liked that because it's not only a marvelous idea but it makes so much sense. I have asked friends of mine who are dancers if they were ever coached like that, and, sadly, they usually say they were not.

Yes, in these modern times, we rarely do, but it was key to Diaghilev, to the way he was taught. In Russia, in the dance school, one is required to study history and painting. In the United States, a dance teacher who tells the student to study painting and sculpture is a rare thing. Diaghilev owned the book *Chorégraphie* by Raoul-Auger Feuillet (published in Paris in 1700) and other period dance treatises and notatated dances. He gave them to Balanchine to use in his ballets. Lo and behold, if you look at any of his pattern-oriented choreography, they are similar to the traditional patterns that were established in the eighteenth century.

What relationships have you found between Baroque dance to the other arts?

I have been noticing that there is a structural proportion common to music, poetry, and dance. For instance, the first four to eight measures of the dance are presentational. They reveal who the character is and why she is there. In reading a poem from that period, the length of the stanza of the poem is comparable to the length of a measure in the dance. I see that the dance was actually a "danced" poem or "mute rhetoric." There is more of a relationship between the acting technique and the dance performance than modern scholars formerly thought. I see how the mask dwells in this art, the more you see the connections to the other arts.

Each of the art forms actually enhances the other; it's entwined.

Yes. I think if you are only working in music, or dance, or theatre, and you fail to recognize the interrelationships of the arts during that time period, you limit yourself in the understanding of the art you are exploring.

Catherine, can you tell me more about the type of visual research that you engage in to help you in the construction and the reconstruction of the images in the work?

I studied a lot of portraits, and especially the work of Natier, a wonderful portrait painter from this time. He portrays women allegorically as Terpsichore or Abundance. When you look at these women in his paintings, they don't have standard eighteenth-century clothes on. They are draped, referring to Greek mythology. There is something so incredible about their eyes. No matter where you stand in the room, they are looking right at you. The pupils of their eyes are dark and exaggerated. When you look at the eyes, there is a brimful of tears, but they are not crying—they are watery.

Do you know why?

Women at that time took belladonna because it made their pupils dilate and gave them a watery look. It was a desired look and was considered beautiful. Then the question for us is, "Why was this beautiful?" When animals are startled or there is some type of sexual arousal or intense interest, the pupils widen. This state is related to compassion, something like the compassionate goddess image; the figure is very beautiful, graceful, and light in motion.

What I find particularly fascinating in Baroque dance is that the gestures have specific meanings. Tell me more about that.

Art in the eighteenth century is symbolic. For instance, any gesture up above refers to the heavens or blessings or happiness. Any gesture that is down has to do with Mother Earth or Hades or the devil or a sense of loss. When you expand those directions to the body moving in space, then you have an expressive structure within which to work, and the choreographer can use these structures to solve choreographic puzzles.

It's as if the dance movements have their own vocabulary and language.

Yes. A knowledge of this gestural lexicon based in the art of declamation gives the choreographer the ability to think in different patterns and not just rely on the inspiration of the moment. It gives us
another standard, another form, another structure to study which is
at the root of Western thought.

Relating rhetoric and declamation to dance choreography began in
the Renaissance and continued to this century through the work of
Delsarte and the early modern dance pioneers like Isadora Duncan,
Ted Shawn, and Doris Humphrey.

Where do you find the creative freedom in the vocabulary?

If you look at ballet choreographers of today, they did not invent
the ballet vocabulary. They use the vocabulary that exists and manip-
ulate it in such a way that they can express themselves. Likewise, I
feel that my talent is in taking the Baroque vocabulary and manipulat-
ing it to create my work.

**What excites you about working in the Baroque style? What is
the attraction for you?**

There is something so beautiful about the way the dances fit with
the music, in a hand-in-glove way, and the abstraction of the floor patterns are just as pleasing as Balanchine's patterns in *Concerto
Barocco.* What I love about dance is the detail. I love coaching the
performer. I love the mathematics of putting certain groups together
and seeing in that abstract form the drama that emerges from it. I
want to use the steps as words; those are my tools. But I don't want
to invent those tools.

**Baroque dance has its limits, but those limits are different
from other forms. Can you speak about how you work with those
limitations?**

As a dancer, when you go into the eighteenth century, it is an in-
trospective journey. It is really a journey of an actress who is dancing.
I was always drawn to dramatic dance, but I was trained to be abstract in my modern and ballet classes. I was pulled into the eighteenth century because I liked the challenge of taking on a character.

Catherine Turocy in costume. *Photograph by Nancy Brooker. Reproduced by permission of Catherine Turocy.*

Even though the movement range was smaller and I didn't understand how to have a full body experience in a small movement range,
I was curious to find out what that would be like.

And what did you discover?

Well, that was the awkwardness and the transition for me, to find
how to pull muscular reflexes in enough and still feel as if I were moving my entire body. It takes at least a year or perhaps two years before you become comfortable in moving in a smaller movement range
and creating the tensions that you have in your body on a more ex-
treme range than in modern dance technique. However, my teacher,
Shirley Wynne, was very patient with me.

How are the dances that you reconstruct notated?

They are recorded in the Feuillet notation system. It differs from
modern notations today, but it is a very graphic system. It follows the
ways in which the legs move; it tells the dancer where to move in
space. It also gives the relationship of the dance steps to the music.
It doesn't give the name of the dance positions, but it actually shows,
in a graphic pattern, how the leg is going out to the side and how it
closes in position. It is extremely logical.

**I know you have reconstructed over a hundred dances from
these early notations. It must be such a pleasure for you to see the
handwritten notation. When you study the notation, how does it
speak to you?**

The first thing I look at is actually the spatial pattern. I see the
notes; I see the steps; I see the pattern and the geometry in space. If
the dance is for a couple, it shows if they are going away from each
other, or if they are coming together, or going to opposite sides of the
room. The pattern reflects the relationship between the two people.
The steps give you the conversation that is going on between them. Of
course, all this is happening along with the music. There is a rush here,
or something is being held back, or there is a very dotted rhythm over
there, or it's extremely swingy over here. That gives one more piece of
information about the dance. It's a puzzle that is eventually solved.

Catherine Turocy in *Les Fête d'Hébé*. Copyright Otto M. Berk.

Have you discovered through your research any famous women choreographers from that time?

There were many more women choreographers and women innovators at the beginning of the century than we are aware of. But those women had a distinct disadvantage because many of them could not write, and if you couldn't write, you couldn't get published. They didn't notate their ballets and they didn't write books on the art of dancing. Most of the publications on the art of dancing were written by men. I would be hard-pressed to name a woman who did publish.

Can you take me through your process of choreographing a work?

First, I listen to the music and I am inspired. My first desire to dance as a child came from the music of my father's violin. When I first started the company, I would improvise and I would get up and move to the music and try to find out what felt natural working with the

music. Then, after Jim and I explored the boundaries of period conven-
tion, I would put my motions into eighteenth-century terminology.

**Can you tell me more about working with Jim and what that is
like for you?**

It was my good fortune to fall in love with James Richman early in
my career. Together we have produced opera/ballets and chamber
music and dance concerts all over the world. His artistry has greatly
influenced and inspired my own musical development as a dancer.

**How do you work with the dancers in the company? Can you de-
scribe the process for me?**

When I am working, sometimes I improvise, but most often I will
lay on my back and close my eyes and visualize what the dance is
like to the music. Then I will write it down in my own way and later
teach it to the dancers. My process differs depending on what the
music is or who the dancers are. If I am making a group dance, I will
sit down and map out the whole piece visually. I will get the sense of
what the geometry is, and I will put the steps into that geometry
based on the rhythm of the music.

**Do you make adjustments in the studio according to the
dancer's bodies?**

I watch what they are doing when I teach the steps to them, and if
I notice instinctively that their bodies want to do something else, I will
change it. I believe that for a solo, one must choreograph for that personal voice, for that individual. You have to taper the dance so it's a
strong statement of that individual dancing. What I don't want is to
have a carbon copy of myself doing the solo.

**Do you like feedback from the dancers when you are working on
a piece? Do you find it helpful, or does it take away from your vision?**

I find that it is not only helpful, but I really want the dancer to feed
into the strength of the dance. I don't want them to feel at odds with
what I am asking them to do. When they are performing, I want them to
feel comfortable and inspired in the moment. I want them to feel as if

they have some type of ownership and they can respond to the choreography when they are performing, adjusting a gesture or the timing.

In the late twentieth century, dancers are seen as "tools of the
choreographer," and that is dangerous. There is a responsibility of
the choreographer to bring out the uniqueness of that individual in
performance.

**You bring up a good point. It seems to me it would be wiser to
bring out the best talents of the dancer to serve the dance. I know
many choreographers want dancers to follow their choreography to
the letter, and the dancer is not encouraged or invited to participate
in the creative process. I wonder, do you think that audiences can
tell the difference if the dancer participated in the process of making the dance?**

Yes, I do think that the audience can tell the difference. When the
choreographer makes the dance for the performer, and the audience
feels that the performer has a certain amount of liberty in the interpretation, there is a spontaneity that exists. I think that not to ask
that of the performer diminishes the power of the performer, and that
I find deadly.

**There are a few myths about Baroque dance that I would like to
address. Some people think that the movements are very stiff.**

It isn't if it is done right. Some reconstructors mistakenly believe
that eighteenth century "contained deportment" means that there
shouldn't be any emotion on the face, but this is absolutely wrong.
The idea of being contained is not that the dancer refrains from emot-
ing but that she holds the "fire" inside. She creates a container for
this passion, and the passion is released or not released as the
music progresses.

What other myths would you like to dispel about Baroque dance?

The general misconception that Baroque dance is a museum
piece and therefore won't be interesting. The belief that "anything
that is not athletic cannot be interesting" is another prejudice we
have to fight. Dance is much more than the highest arabesque or the

biggest jeté. Our movement range is on the smaller end of the scale, so we are immediately looking at a more filigreed and detailed work, much as the other visual arts of that period—the paintings, sculpture, furniture, and architecture—had that type of detail and filigree.

When you are wearing the mask and you are portraying a certain character, how do you convey certain emotions?

The mask depersonalizes the performer. When I am wearing the mask, I am not Catherine Turocy under that mask, I am Venus or Diana. When I say it depersonalizes, what I mean is that it allows me to take my own identity and put it to the side. It allows me to take that sense of who Venus is and to put that into my body. Through the mask, I am able to speak and to portray Venus, or whoever it is that I am portraying. The mask is not a disguise; the mask is not something that restricts expression—it frees expression. In Eastern dance, especially in Indian or Balinese dance, they feel that the dancer is actually taking on "that spirit," and that spirit possesses the body.

In the Western tradition, for the eighteenth century, it is somewhat similar, but it is not that you are possessed. As an artist, one understands that the dance is an interpretation of Venus, and the dancer is able to relay who that woman is while wearing her mask. Since the mask hides the wearer's face, the dancer can put her own face aside, her own identity aside, and take on the identity of Venus.

How is the dancer's intellectual and physical intelligence used in the performance?

My being becomes a puppet. I am at once both the puppet and the puppeteer. When you put the mask on, it makes the whole body a doll. It makes the whole body a living sculpture that can be formed into different gestures and different dynamics. The dance steps reveal the character through the mask.

It must be a lovely freedom for you as the performer.

It is very liberating feeling as a performer inside the mask because I can be somebody I am not. It is also liberating for the audience because they realize *you* are not there. They see this face on the mask, and when it is donned by the dancer, the whole body becomes a puppet or a doll. When the audience is looking at the face, they look at it to find out "What is she thinking?" "Who is she?" Because she is going to convey this through her face and because we are accustomed to looking at people's faces, as soon as the face is taken away and replaced by the mask, they say to themselves, "I don't have to look at the mask. I see the mask. I see what it says. I see who it is. I see that it is a face that has a certain attitude, but it is not going to change because it is a mask. Now, I have to look at the whole body." Somehow, it forces the audience to look at the dancer's entire body.

Can you explain more about the image of your body as "puppet"?

When they see my entire body, that is when I become this expressive puppet. To become a living puppet behind this mask is, in a way, an ultimate freedom, because any nuance that I do with any part of my body is seen and perceived by the audience. It's a contradiction in a way. The mask hides my face but it reveals my identity. And in the performances, the mask itself seems to change.

What happens to you when you take the mask off? Can you return to yourself immediately or does that take time? When does the self reenter the body?

Mainly, it's a matter of breathing. When going through a tense, emotional state, the breathing changes, and that happens with the mask. When I make that transition from the stage to the dressing room, somehow I become myself again. The breathing steadies, and then the mask comes off. Rarely do I shed the mask right after I come off the stage. I usually wait until I get to the dressing room and then I take it off.

Have you ever been lost in the process?

Once I was dancing for students at Santa Monica College and I only had on my practice clothes. Because I didn't have to run to the dressing room to change, I didn't have the time that I usually need. As I was preparing to speak to them, I took the mask off and there was a moment of transition when I felt incredibly vulnerable. I wanted to cry. It's like being that little crustacean without your shell. You are molting and you are waiting for the next shell to come on and it hadn't arrived yet.

Can you describe to me how that felt?

I took my mask off, and Catherine Turocy, the person who was lecturing, hadn't arrived yet. I was that performer who was somewhere between having just interpreted a role and looking for myself. It was such a strong feeling of being lost and feeling really sad. When I took my mask off, it was a very vulnerable state to be in. It shocked me into the fact that you have to pay attention to these transitions. The mask is powerful; it does allow you to experience a part of life in a realm that doesn't exist. Yet the mask exists very strongly. It is a metaphysical state.

Can you describe that "metaphysical state" to me?

I experience in my physical sensation of performing a very rehearsed release of energy that has a shape to it; it has a rhythm and a dynamic. It is very odd to talk about dance as metaphysical because it is so physical, but when that release of energy is artfully released, I experience the sound of music and the visual flow of a line in sculpture.

Is it a heightened kinesthetic sense?

It is a kinesthetic sense, but it is also not physical; it is an ideal. Imagine that you are a puppeteer and making a puppet move. It's a physical experience for you moving the puppet, but you aren't actually jumping or leaping; the puppet is when you are wearing your mask. Your body becomes the puppet and your mind is separated from that body. Your mind is telling you to do these things, and you do it because you are both the puppet and puppeteer.

I am curious to know how that feels in the body. I don't think I can compare that to anything I have ever experienced.

It's as if you are in suspended time. The time is infinite and it's short at the same moment. It's a very odd experience. Remember, for every minute of dance seen on stage, there are four hours of rehearsal behind it. So when that minute is going by, the performer has those four hours of experience happening to her simultaneously because everything worked on prior to the performance is now coming through. It's a very wild feeling. It's a state of being that doesn't exist anywhere else for me except on the stage.

The sense of time is also different in Baroque dancing. How does that sense of time feel?

If you look at Baroque art, let's say a painting by Boucher or Watteau, and take a corner of that painting and cut it out, you could make a postcard because there is so much detail. In dance, each phrase is packed with small detail and filigreed motion because the dancer is not taking four measures in triple meter music to go from a standing position into a nice, long, luxurious arabesque. On the contrary, in eighteenth-century choreography the dancer has at least two or three changes of weight per measure, and every once in a while, six changes per measure. It feels dense. It feels like Godiva chocolates.

Do you have any particular rituals when you perform?

If you want to be dramatic, there is a sense of ritual about the rehearsal and getting to that moment of performance, like the sacrifice. The actual sense of performance of that piece doesn't exist in time or space because it is much more than the current time and space.

Catherine, do you think that your talents as a dancer and choreographer are a "gift"?

I do believe it's a gift, and there is a responsibility with that gift. You can't ignore that gift. I think it is God-given. It's like opening a door, and you can't pretend that you didn't open that door.

Have your dreams ever helped you choreograph?

Sometimes when I am choreographing, I am in a half-dream state, and if I am very tired, it turns into a dream. In 1978, I was under a deadline and trying to sleep. I was thinking a lot about my choreography, and I started visualizing what different sections would look like. I went through the entire concert, and I choreographed it in my head. When I awoke the next morning, I just wrote down the structure and the outline for the dances. I was able to finish the choreography the next day.

It's a mysterious process. What I find particularly compelling is how different the creative process is.

There is a mystery to it, and there is a realization that if you can envision it, and think it, you probably can do it. It gives ideas much more of a weightier sense. They just aren't in this world yet, but they do exist.

Have you ever had doubts about your work, perhaps at the beginning of your career?

The one nice thing about being young and optimistic is that you don't have any doubts. You have to be mature to have doubts. I didn't think about doubts though; I just thought I would go out there and do my best and people would like it. I was so taken by the Baroque dance style and I knew that I loved it, so why wouldn't everybody else love it? Those doubts didn't actually creep in until after the company existed for about ten years.

I think when you are the person creating the choreography and you are putting your life into that, you may have doubts about a decision, about administration or finances, but never really about the art.

Do you believe that "one is born a dancer"?

I do. I know that many, many dancers feel it's their calling. There is this feeling that they *have* to dance. It's a calling, indeed. I always knew. I told my mother I was going to be a dancer when I was four years old.

What were you like as a child?

I was quiet. But there were a couple of telltale things, though. If a child gets frustrated easily and cries a lot, she may be an artist. I think my first ballet teacher, Miss Betsey, thought I was an abused child because I cried in every technique class I had whenever I couldn't do exactly what it was she was showing us to do. I had to work

Catherine Turocy as a child in ballerina costume. *Photographer unknown.*
Reproduced by permission of Catherine Turocy.

hard at it. When you are small, you learn to crawl, walk, and talk. Dancing was yet another language to learn. I hated making mistakes. I couldn't accept that I could do something wrong.

Are you still a perfectionist?

I am a perfectionist, but I see it as a process. It took a while to get to that understanding. There is a desire to be perfect. It is perfection when you are with every moment as it passes and you play that. It's an intended aliveness during the performance. The aim is not to have a perfect performance but to go out there and be as alive as you can possibly be.

What about stage fright? Have you ever experienced it?

When I was in grade school and high school, I loved dancing but I didn't like performing because I was too self-conscious. I was in a ballet company from age twelve to eighteen, but there was not *one* performance that I enjoyed, although I felt this need to perform. I decided that if I got through college and I still didn't like performing, I would quit dancing. But there was this other part of me that told me I had to perform.

What happened in college that changed things for you?

In my freshman year of college at Ohio State University, I was fortunate enough to work with Lynn Dally who taught our improvisation class. It was through her class that I understood more of what it was that I loved about the dance. You are in an act of creation when you are improvising. I realized that when I was performing, I was not in the act of creation. I was in the act of mimicking motions that I was asked to perform, that someone else had imposed on my body. Eventually, I understood that as an interpretive artist, you have to create in the moment, while you are performing, otherwise you aren't being true to the choreographer.

Do you believe that there is a palpable energy that exists when you are performing in front of different audiences?

Yes. You can feel it if there is a little bit of light. If you make contact with them and they make it back with you, you have a conversation going on as you perform.

Are you concerned about the future of Baroque dance?

Yes. I am concerned about the future of dance in general. Baroque dance needs very talented choreographers and performers, but the difficulty with Baroque dance is that we need artists who are talented as performers/choreographers/reconstructors who also have an appreciation for the scholarly research that can be applied to the performance. That is why I continue to teach. We need the dance equivalent of someone like Kenneth Branaugh to become involved. I would love to teach him a minuet.

5

Alonzo King

"In his choreography, one always sees his passion for classical movement for its own sake. For contrast, he will juxtapose formal phrases with modern-dance elements like torso contractions and angular and stilted movements. Balanchine's influence shows up in the formalistic way he moves groups and in the deeply romantic nature of his pas de deux. 'For me,' King says, 'choreography is a language that communicates more clearly than the language of words. My ballets—all a continuation of one another—are my song.'"

———Valerie Gladstone, *The New York Times,* 1998

Alonzo King. *Copyright Marty Sohl. Courtesy of LINES Contemporary Ballet.*

Dance speaks a universal language, and Alonzo King has both the ability and the privilege to make that language decipherable. His choreography pries open the heart, and there is something so ancient, so primitive in his works that perhaps explains why his admirers are drawn to it. Whenever I watch his choreography performed by his San Francisco–based LINES Company (where he is artistic director), I feel washed clean, as if I have just engaged in a powerful and prayerful ritual. He has the unique sensibility to turn the theatre into a sanctuary, echoing dance's earliest intention.

King unites his choreographic signatures of elegance and precision with the divine elements; thus one cannot dismiss the sacred aspects of his choreography because they are integral to the man and his choreography. For example, in *String Trio,* the dancers move inside intricately and delicately shaped forms, gliding through the mood-lifting and serene score by the Moses Sedler Group. Watching *Trio,* it was easy to imagine that the dancers weaving in and out of both elevated and flat pointe were goddesses who jumped from a centuries-old urn to celebrate Spirit.

King's devotion is rooted in his ceaseless exploration for the divine in movement. He has studied Eastern and Western mystical thought, Jungian psychology, and the words of the saints and sages. His choreography breathes the majesty of the sacred, embued with knowledge that can only be learned from personal reflection and contemplation. He told me,

> Classical ballet is not a style, but a science that is rooted in universal principles. They are the same principles that have informed science and folklore since time. Neither is an invention. It is a discovery like in all truths.

Growing up in a variety of locations including Georgia, California, Ohio, and New York, he was tremendously inspired by his parents. "I was incredibly influenced by my parents. My mother always encouraged me to be creative, to draw, to write, and to communicate. It was never, ever denied." Through the eyes of a child, he witnessed performances of dance and music in the home, keenly observing and learning about the arts of other cultures. His parents

divorced, but King's relationship with his father, Slater King, a
noted civil rights activist and a prominent businessman, was a close
one. Tenderly, he described him as "a man with a glow." King
learned firsthand about human rights, frequently attending civil-
rights demonstrations with his father.

When he was of college age, he was offered several scholarships
but chose to attend Fisk University in Tennessee because he was
frustrated with being the "only black person in an all-white school
and I wanted to change that." After a semester of study, he answered the "call" to dance and spent the next few years studying
dance on full scholarship at the Harkness School of Ballet, Alvin
Ailey's Dance School, and American Ballet Theatre, where he
worked with the brilliant teacher Stanley Williams.

He performed in Europe, dancing with several European companies, and after a year abroad he returned to New York City.
After a brief apprenticeship with the Alvin Ailey Dance Company,
he left to study with one of his mentors, Bella Lewitzky. King also
performed with the companies of Donald McKayle, Lucas Hoving,
and the Harkness Youth Company.

Realizing that becoming a choreographer was his "highest intention," King formed LINES Contemporary Ballet in San Francisco in
1982. Reexamining the dance training that he had received and recognizing the training that was lacking for dancers, he fashioned a
holistic approach that would nurture all the aspects of a dancer's
persona: mind, body, and spirit. Oddly enough, his approach is one
of the best-kept secrets in the dance world. He explained:

> In my training as a dancer, I found that there were two
> things that were missing. One was the spiritual force and
> the other was the concept that "it is within you," so that the
> idea of training would be to bring "it" out or to remove the
> obstacles to do "it." In the majority of dance training that I
> have observed in Western dance, the idea was that you did
> not have "it," and you must emulate and imitate these out-
> side forces to get "it." Most training is built on the assump-
> tion that to know anything, we have to come to it from the
> outside. We have "to do" instead of "be."

Obvious to anyone who has seen his company perform is King's approach to dance. He combines the metaphysical and physical aspects of dance, emphasizing both the visceral and conceptual intelligence inherent inside each dancer. King is able to call upon the dancer's creative soul by drawing up and excavating their talents. Such physical honesty invites an audience to experience the power of his choreography, not only with the head but with the heart. All that is required for that understanding is an active and alert receptivity. I am convinced that his work is winged.

His innovative dance training, combining the forces from within and without, has earned him great respect, beckoning many dancers who desire much more than technical mastery. William Forsythe, the artistic director for the Frankfurt Ballet, described King as "One of the few ballet masters of our times. His choreography is rich with the complex refractions that demonstrate a full command of the art's intricacies."

Word-of-mouth is the standard operative for artists finding King, since he keeps a low profile. He is usually discovered by synchronistic occurrences. His talents were recognized by prima ballerina Natalia Markarova, when she chose him to coach her for her roles in *Eugene Onegin* and *Swan Lake*. Actor Patrick Swayze saw one of his pieces (*Lila*) and was so impressed that he sought him out to work with him on a film project. Gerald Arpino, artistic director for the Joffrey Ballet, walked into his studio, watched a rehearsal, and immediately invited him to choreograph for his company.

In recognition for his choreographic talents, he has received an NEA Choreographer's Fellowship and a National Dance Residency Award. King has served on panels for the National Endowment for the Arts, the California Arts Council, the City of Columbus Arts Council, and the Lila Wallace Reader's Digest Arts Partnership Program. He was also arts commissioner for the city and county of San Francisco.

His ballets are in the repertory of Ballet Frankfurt, Dresden Ballet, Ballet Met, Washington Ballet, Joffrey Ballet, the Hong Kong Ballet, Dance Theatre of Harlem, North Carolina Dance Theater, and Dallas Black Dance Theater. As a master teacher, he has taught classes for San Francisco Ballet, Lés Ballets de Monte Carlo, Ballet Rambert, National Ballet of Canada, and the North Carolina School of the Arts. He has also collaborated with masters in the world of music, including Pharoah Sanders, Hamza El Din, Berniece Johnson Reagon, and Zakir Hussain.

When I met with King, I was struck by his total focus, generosity, and depth of conversation. It was far more than words, and a conversation that I will always remember.

You have worked with many dancers, Alonzo, some famous and some who have not yet achieved stardom. Can you speak about what moves you, what touches you when you work with a dancer?

There are so many extraordinary dancers that the majority of the world doesn't get to see. Originals. Dancers who develop themselves and often work in obscure places, some by choice and others by circumstance, but dancing fiercely because they must. It's always inspiring for me to come across those artists.

Enthusiasm is the main quality to bring to the work process, because I believe that in that mental state everything is possible. Childlike trust is also wonderful, when the dancer is open and willing, and is without caution or judgment and follows your lead. It's also great to witness strong will and character in a dancer, or watch the process of character being built or the will being strengthened. It's always moving to watch something in transformation.

When I see someone grappling with a physical or a mental obstacle, whether it is some personal psychological kink or mastering a technical demand, it is uplifting to witness them overcome obstacles and reach their objective. It affirms the power of thought and energy to dissolve limitation and make things possible.

What was it like for you to work with Natalia Markarova? How did she find you?

Working with Natalia was like working with an ideal. Her knowledge and understanding of the art is so deep that she was always drenched in quality and conviction. I never had to "pull" anything out of her—it was always there. The principle focus of our rehearsals was mechanics. When I was at American Ballet Theatre School, she had just defected from Russia and was dancing for ABT, and I was always moved by her performances. Long after I had relocated to San Francisco, she walked into the studio after hearing about me from a masseur, stood in the doorway, and said, "Will you work for me?" I said, "Are you kidding?", and I began to coach her for *Eugene Onegin, Swan Lake,* and *Raymonda* for performances she was specifically doing with the Royal and National Ballet of Canada and ABT. It was a serious time, and we worked closely and intensely, and also laughed a lot.

Was her stature as a famous dancer at all intimidating for you?

The wonderful thing about work is that once you get started, you don't think about a person's stature or lack of it, because the focus is the work and what must be accomplished. It's liberating. The setting up of an ideal and the maneuvering of how to get there. Natalia has such a deep understanding of dance and music. It was a real learning experience for me in so many ways. During that time, she asked me to create a solo for her called *Aprés un Revu,* which was a blast.

You also worked with Patrick Swayze. What was it like to work with him?

It always astonishes me when I see Hollywood retrospectives revealing the number of actors who began as dancers. Patrick began as a dancer. His mother had a dance school and company in Texas. He also danced with the Harkness Ballet, and understudied Baryshnikov while he was with Eliot Feld's Ballet Company. Patrick is intelligent, passionate, and powerful.

How did you meet?

He attended a Joffrey performance and saw a ballet I set called *Lila,* starring Valerie Madonia, a beautiful dancer. Patrick and his wife, Lisa (who is also a wonderful dancer), were blown away by Valerie's performance and went backstage. They asked her about me, and Patrick told Valerie he wanted to meet me and asked for my phone number. Later,

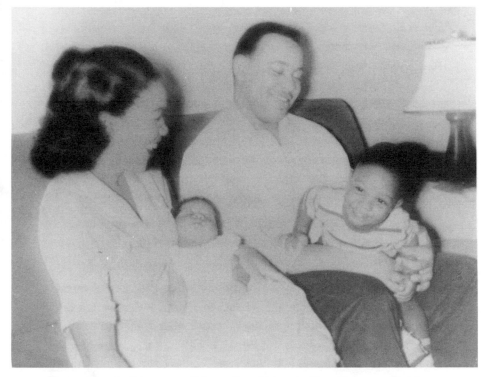

Alonzo King in the arms of his mother, Valencia King Nelson, with his father, Slater King, and brother, Slater King, Jr. *Courtesy of LINES Contemporary Ballet.*

Patrick and Lisa invited me to go to Los Angeles to work on a movie they were making. We worked really hard and had a really good time.

Alonzo, what I enjoy about watching your work, and what always engages me is the details, the filigree work—a point of the toe, a turn of the hip. These really intricate and small gestures are riveting and very compelling. I attended a performance with a friend who hadn't seen your choreography, and I told him not to try to look at the big picture. I told him that wherever his eye would gaze was the place to look, and to trust that. Many of these subtle movements are not decorative, and sometimes they aren't pretty, but they are stunning. When you are choreographing, is this detail work a conscious process or do you "see" the details later on?

When you first get an idea, it is usually crude and undigested, and you need time for assimilation and reflection. While the work is being constructed you observe the dancers' understanding of movement ideas. When the ideas become clear and the language understood, you begin to attract an inner response. When you have studied or observed anything closely and given it deep thought, you begin to understand its nature. You begin to understand the inner workings and motivation, the obvious and subtle responses of movement character. The awareness becomes heightened because of your attention, because you are becoming what you are observing. Often after building a work, you view the primary essence, hone it for clarity, and give it more fragrance.

That's a lovely phrase, "to give it fragrance." Have you always had the kind of eye you have now? When you were a child, did you always notice the nuances of things?

I'm sure the details of my childhood that I remember seem larger in retrospect. The eye is nothing without the mind. We really see with the mind. As mental understanding increases we are able to see more. You know, the expression "Well, the way I see it . . ." is really about comprehension and understanding. But our senses are limited and can fool the mind, thus inferential reasoning is really shaky ground. Intuition is indisputable because it is direct perception.

There is a state where you can know things by feeling. The language of vibration is much more real than words. Without looking you can see. This ability is very strong in children, but with age and conditioning this ignored faculty becomes weak, because like any ability it has to be trained and strengthened or it will weaken from lack of use. People begin to doubt the part of them that "just knows."

You mean intuition? Can you speak more about that?

Intuition is usually an underdeveloped muscle because most of us are taught to concentrate on the instruments that measure things from the outside. The real knowing is intuitive. Unfortunately, in art classes children are trained to draw what they see, instead of what they mean. Our educational system is usually devoid of nature and suffocates individuality.

So the eye takes over as we get older?

Yes. A young child's inner world is quite strong. There are many interior gifts that are abandoned when materialism and doubt begin to take a stronger hold on the child's mind, and the ratio of feeling and intellect is tilted predominately towards logic. As the abrasions from the obstacles in the world begin to take their toll, we lose our freshness and harden. We have to work to keep the mind pliable and elastic.

My cognitive sense feels sharper now in its ability to conceive exterior form, but there was a sense of knowing that has no relation to the outside world that is not as strong as when I was a child. Nevertheless, if you spend a long time devoted to something, it will begin to speak to you and reveal its secrets, and the real form behind its guise will become clear. The true knowing of one subject opens the door to the understanding of so many things.

Do you mean based on your years of experience as a dancer and choreographer?

Yes, and based on experience and reflection. Watching the work. Relentless inquiry. Asking the tough questions. "What is the truth behind appearance and what animates these forms, and can it be isolated and shown? When is a gesture so steeped in honesty that it is universally recognizable and understood?"

It seems like one needs a combination of skills for that knowledge to be present: a well-developed eye, years of experience, and the ability to listen to one's internal dialogue.

Yes, and also from that internal listening, you understand how all things are related. Understanding when science becomes poetry and physics becomes religion. It's understanding the divine model, understanding the universal principle for all making and doing that everything is based upon.

Were you encouraged as a child to pay attention to your internal prompting and speak about it?

Yes. I was encouraged to cultivate the positive ones because I had a lot of internal promptings that were not so positive. My parents were incredibly supportive and encouraged whatever I was interested in that was positive. I think it's important to maintain that privacy of the inner world. At an early age, I was exposed to art of many cultures. My mother was attending university when I was a child, and people from around the world would come to our house and share the music and the dance of their cultures. That left a deep impression on me.

I remember when you told me about the time your stepfather took you to your first ballet, and after the performance you gave him a complete critique.

I was about eight years old. The curtain opened and it seemed so familiar, but there wasn't the awe of newness at all. After the performance I had all these criticisms about how it should have been done, what was done poorly, and who was OK, etc. It really annoyed him.

Is that when you knew you would become a dancer/ choreographer?

No, it wasn't then when I knew, but I think I saw clearly and understood what was missing from the performance.

As a child, did you know you would be involved in the dance world?

As a child, I never thought of wanting to be a dancer. I just danced all the time, everywhere and anywhere. My mother would dance with me and she always encouraged it.

Can you give me an example of someone whose dancing really affected you?

My mother's dancing really affected me. But I think the first time I was awestruck by theatrical dance was watching the performance of an astonishing female artist in Eleo Pomare's company in a solo called *Hex*. I felt as though I has seen real dance as it should be. It was amazing.

When did you *know* when this would be your life?

At the end of high school, I had to make a decision as to what I would be able to do for a long time and enjoy. What could I really commit myself to? Dance has always consistently given me the most joy.

Can you speak about other influences on you when you were a child besides your mother?

My mother's character has a very strong influence on me. Her privacy, courage, subtlety, depth of conviction, and her dancing were doctrines that have taken me more than my childhood to assimilate.

Early in my childhood, I attended parochial school, and the church and some of the clergy have had a strong affect on me. I was an altar boy and really enjoyed learning the Latin for Mass, the symmetry and beauty of the altar, the serving, the whole thing. I was so into it. I always volunteered to do the private Mass for the nuns at 6 am and the regular Mass for the students at 7 am.

Was it the ritualistic elements that you liked?

Yes, I loved that part of it, but there were other things. The faces of some of the older parishioners were like camouflaged majesty. They appeared to be anchored in stillness like rocks, and their countenance was luminous.

I liked the idea of service, the formality of a direction, that certain things were done at a certain time. The idea of transformation, the symbolism everywhere, it all spoke to me of service and conviction.

I liked being in an environment that was seemingly another world—with beautiful architecture, music, order, peace, and devotion. The Eucharist transubstantiation was for me the entire exegesis for the practice of art. It was a rite, and from the experience of that rite a person should be changed. That this was not merely bread and wine but truly the body and blood of Christ also meant that all symbols and signs were physical and psychological means for spiritual transport.

I was reading about your dad and his work as an activist for human rights and his work as a humanitarian. He must have been an extraordinary person. I would like you to tell me more about him and his influence in your life.

He was an unusual man. He sang his own song. He was ambitious and had a steady enthusiasm. He liked himself and he loved people. He was a successful businessman in Georgia and president of the Albany Movement, a civil-rights organization in the 1960s. He traveled the world, lectured on land and human reform, and was instrumental in selling large parcels of land in the south to African-Americans in the north inspired by a movement called "Land is Power." The movement believed that without land, you had nothing. He was also close friends with Malcom X; in fact, a large part of their correspondence was given to the Fisk University Library.

What did you learn from him?

My father introduced me to meditation and showed by his example that your life should be authentic. At that time, people had a real cause; the fight for civil rights, and what people preached and believed in was an actual part of their lives. My father went to jail many times. He took my brother and me to marches with him. He lived what he believed in. He was vibrant and original.

In your piece *Rock,* you use gospel music as a background. Was that choice directly influenced by your father and his work?

In a way it was, because as a child, I remember Berniece Reagon, the director of *Sweet Honey in the Rock,* singing at Mass meetings when she was a teenager, and being wowed by the power of the meetings and her voice. I wanted to work with her for some time.

On the other hand, the work is about human experience. Anything that happens to anyone affects everyone in the same way. We are now recognizing our ecological responsibility and connectedness to all inhabitants of this planet. Most of us view things through the prism of our own consciousness. If you are a political person, that is your take on things; if you are drenched in moneymaking, that is how you view things; if you are a feminist, you see things from that aspect.

It's your filter. Alonzo, do you think that the artist's role is to inform people much like a poet does, to name things?

The artist's role is accuracy. The artist is the same as the scientist or truth-seeker relentlessly searching for the *X* factor, the common denominator, or the truth that lies behind all that is transitory, the engineer and investigator into the "how to make and do" of all of that is to be made and done. In this search, every conception must be no less than pulverized, to discover if it is based in the timelessness of truth. What should be done takes precedence over what one wants to do. The idea of yourself becomes annihilated and the goal alone exists. Only what is permanent and essential matters. There is nothing that can be well made without the use of art.

Are you concerned with the way that audiences perceive your choreography? Is it important to you for them to "get it"?

Yes, because the point after all is communication. Too often we view art in terms of taste and sentiments (likes and dislikes), how it looks and makes us feel, our reactions to it, as opposed to what is being said, contemplating its exactness or distortion. The myths, images, lines, and symbols are all words that have meaning. Dance is, after all, a language, and we certainly wouldn't expect an orator to go to the podium and babble senselessly. The facts reveal something.

The popular belief is that art is an affair of emotional whim and indulgence. You often hear people say, "The only thing that matters about art is what you like." Do we, then, think that the only thing that matters about diet is what tastes good to us, or the only thing that matters about conduct is what feels good to us? So why should art be irrational? Art is related to law, an intellectual virtue, the knowledge of how things are done—whether that art is raising children, making food, or creating dances.

When people are swept up in the colors and textures, that is a good thing, but those things are a lure, an attraction, or a summons to something other than itself. You know the Buddhist metaphor of the finger pointing to the moon and everyone is looking at the finger? The worship of these symbols becomes idolatrous; it is what the symbols refer to that is the point. The mystical sense is contained in the literal.

You often use the phrase "to be in service to the art form," and of your desire for the dancers in your company "to be in service to the work." Can you comment on what you meant by that?

The artist/dancer is not an exhibitionist, or looking to display him-

self/herself or personality; they are solely concerned with communicating ideas clearly. The dancer's first and primary duty is to radiate,
like the sun. To work is to do something; to serve is to become something. It is much more enjoyable to "be" instead of to "do." Ideally,
the dancer really wants to be "danced" rather than to dance.

The first place we get stuck is identification with the body. The
dancer is really "playing" the body as a musical instrument by manip-
ulating the energies to express ideas. For the most part, the body is
usually a disappointing tool for the limitless realms that are going on

Alonzo King in dance rehearsal. *Copyright Marty Sohl. Courtesy of LINES
Contemporary Ballet.*

in the dancer's mind. When the vessel is empty, the Spirit enters. Most of us are double- or even triple-minded, looking in one direction with the mind and saying one thing and really meaning something else. When you witness someone who is single-minded, it is very powerful. The dancer has to be single-focused in action.

We have spoken about this before, Alonzo. I would like you to comment on your beliefs that the work comes from a higher source? How does that process take place for you?

Technically, everything comes from a higher source. As we have discussed before, it's all a matter of degrees, as Spirit is everything. The hierarchy is mind over matter, soul over mind. Our mind is the tip of an inverted pyramid that has no base, which reaches into infinity. We have our ordinary mind, our subconscious mind, and the super-conscious mind, which is the vault of all knowledge and power.

All great thoughts, all invention, is acquired through the supercon-scious mind. The world's great composers, inventors, saints, scien-tists, and reformers acknowledge tapping into that source. It is accessible to everyone; there is no ownership of ideas. It takes place by being still and entering a place of keen interest with deep concen-tration, or by great faith. I attended a lecture where a brilliant soul was speaking, and he stated that dance began by people imitating sages in exalted states of ecstasy.

That is a very rich image.

When we admire landscapes, there is something behind those landscapes that is moving us. When we are moved by babies, there is something behind those babies that is moving us. It is Spirit. It is in-escapable. You've heard the expression the "life" of a work, meaning that it's animated by some force, living and breathing. So it follows that a work without life is dead, lifeless. It is Spirit alone that gives life. We can stuff a dead body with all the most vital nutrients that the world has to offer, but that doesn't bring life.

You are really speaking about aspects of the invisible world, a world that does exist but is not seen. It is felt.

All matter is addressing that. Yes, we all want to make the invisible visible. Whether that is accessing character or seeing behind things to what they really are. Dancing is about Spirit. We forget that design, construction, logic, and form is also Spirit.

Is it a matter of accessing divine knowledge to use in the creative process? Can you speak more about that process?

Electricity has always been here, but relatively recently discovered, and it will continue that way, discovery after discovery, until as Yogananda says, "The impossible will eventually become the inevitable."

Balanchine said, "We reassemble." We don't make anything, we discover, because its all there. Ballet too was discovered. The term *ballet*, which is the Italian word for *dance,* is really a misnomer when used to connote what would be properly called Western classical dance. The classical ideal is represented in all great civilizations. All civilizations copied models by looking back to what was considered before them as the Golden Age. Europe looked back to ancient Rome. Rome looked to Greece. Greece looked to Egypt. Egypt looked to India. Invention is really a metaphysical principle applied to practical end. All true folklore and fairy tales are filled with metaphysical principles.

Can you give me an example?

You've often heard that the greatest invention was the wheel. Ancient man also looked to the divine symbols in nature for his instructions, "As above, so below." Contemplatives watching the sun in its daily journey was the cause for the invention of the wheel. It's hard for us who live in cities to imagine the enormous impact that the presence of nature has in informing the lives of those who have listened to her. Because we are so disintegrated, it's also difficult for us to think that something can fulfill a function and also express a meaning.

In *Swan Lake,* Siegfried is not a young prince who fell in love with a bird. This is a person who is at the crossroads and must make a choice between Spirit and matter. A choice must be made between all that is comfortable and expected and required for his station in life, or the "white bird," which is cross-culturally a symbol of Spirit. He makes a promise of fidelity to this cause and is betrayed by matter, represented by the Black Swan. You find the same stories in the folk-lore of every culture.

Although, I think that our culture is changing dramatically. It seems that many people are reluctant to accept the idea of Spirit in their lives; it's unfamiliar and threatening. Why do you think that is?

It seems that for most of us any thing, person, or idea that we haven't taken the time to know is going to seem odd at first. You have to have some interest to make the time to know Spirit, just like anything else. It is something that has to be experienced. It can't be understood through matter. The experience of Spirit is so personal and for the most part secretive, and understandably so. It's an inner experience, and to talk about it is to lessen it.

Can it be articulated?

Oh, yes, saints and sages around the world have articulated it profoundly in every detail. But it is still something that has to be experienced personally. It is a private journey.

Can you speak about the sacred aspects in your work which is so apparent?

Apparent to you. It depends on how you are looking.

You can't miss it. It knocks you over. I love that element in your work.

Everyone has a different take. I think it's in all work. Practicality and good construction are certainly sacred. You know the result of art is your child and has a mixture of both the physical and the spiritual.

I watch a great deal of dance, and often a lot of performances are disappointing. I think that the dancers in your company are not only gorgeous and well trained, but they know how to dance your choreography, work that is soulful and moving to me. It's choreography that makes me think, and I really like that.

Thank you. I really appreciate that.

Alonzo, how do you coach your dancers? Do you use symbols or

paintings or other arts besides dance?

You can point to paintings, books, and locations, all of which are great and useful, but the true search is within. Things can only be known personally.

"He is best educated to whom all that he sees and hears conveys its lessons." When someone who has known something becomes something, there is clarity.

Clarity or light helps us all. The illumination from great dancing can change lives. The key thing is understanding. The movement has to be realized. To give language power, the person speaking must know fully what they are talking about. You may hear two different speakers saying the exact same thing, using the exact same words, and one will strike you motionless and the other will be hardly noticed and soon forgotten. It is because the former has experienced and fully realized what they are saying, and the latter is just reciting words with proper elocution and speaking techniques but without understanding. Understanding usually comes after a state of heightened awareness. That awareness always begins with the self.

If you are a farmer, you don't necessarily have to leave the farm to get educated. You begin your observations wherever you are. A state of elevated awareness enlightens what you are contemplating, whether that is yourself, your work, or what is around you.

It begins with the axiom "know thyself." Now, this proposes an endless chain of questions, one of which is "Who am I?" This interrogation shucks layers of false or temporary identifications like race, gender, occupation, and on and on, until you ultimately arrive at Spirit.

At the dance studio, there is a daily examination of what the purpose of being there is, the understanding of the body in its relation to the mind and the soul, the origins of form and their meaning, and what uniqueness we are bringing to the art.

When you have finished a work and it has been performed, do you feel as if it is complete or do you try to make it better?

If a change would make an idea clearer, of course I would do it. And, yes, there are some works that are built on the particular strength and understanding of a dancer, and often when that dancer goes, so does the work.

Are you hard on yourself when you watch a performance? Is it complete for you when it is performed?

If what I intended to do was done, it is finished. If I have missed the mark, then it isn't finished. But I always think it could be better. Everything we do is really an opportunity.

Do you ever watch the audience? What are you searching for?

Sometimes I do. Often when I sit in the audience to watch the performance, I am aware of the periods when the room becomes still and when it loses focus. During intermissions, it's sometimes interesting to be anonymous and hear the comments.

Audiences are so different on any given night, and sometimes the response has nothing to do with the choreography, but it may reflect the people in the room that evening and their moods.

Sometimes it's hard to tell. An audience can be really "there" and show little response, and vice versa. But what I am really looking at is how the dancers are working, if they are growing, if I see change in them, if the generosity is always increasing and they are giving more each time. Because it is a responsibility. They are not doing routines; they are radiating. If that is happening, then I know it's OK.

When you are choreographing, do you prefer to be very clear about what you want to accomplish first, or do you like to tinker and see what comes? What is your creative process like?

When I choreograph for other companies, I am usually under so much pressure to produce in short amounts of time that I have to be as clear as possible. My preference is to take a lot of time and explore.

Do you get that time?

Rarely, but that's my preference. I usually have that opportunity with LINES. But there have been several occasions when I've had to produce a work in one week.

Is there any pleasure for you when you work under time constraints?

It can be a rush, but it can also wear you out. It depends on your drive, stamina, and fertility at that time.

Do your dreams influence you at all?

They used to, years ago, and I really relished that, but I don't seem to be having dreams much these days. Now the primary focus is hard work and good dance-building.

Do you have specific rituals that you like to do before you begin a new work?

First, I figure out what is needed and then I search for music and spend a lot of time alone.

Do you move or mostly sit?

I take walks, move, and sit; I do all of that. But mostly I listen; I am quiet and then I move.

What would you advise a young choreographer about learning the craft?

To watch how nature works. To observe the form in great music, architecture, and literature of all cultures. To notice the broad construction of every kind of "making": ant hills, bridges, brooms. Make as many dances as you can while you can. But the most important thing is to spend time in thought and reflection about who you are. It is important to discover the reality of things and not their appearance, so what is made can have a true form as its reference.

Would you advise them to study choreography in school?

I would advise that first they gain a discipline in one form of dance and then learn as many other forms as they can. Study the masters, seek out a solid craftsperson, or apprentice with someone whose work you admire. Look at the work until you can understand what is being said.

We can learn about formula and design, but the real work has to be discovered and, more importantly, understood alone. Thought is incredibly powerful. Everything begins with thought. We become what we think most about.

How do you do that? How do you tune in to yourself?

By focusing on one thing at a time. To be able to empty yourself and just tune in. That is really what is meant by the phrase "to walk in someone else's shoes." To hear and become them. Remember, the Spirit enters when the vessel is empty. We have to get out of the way. The biggest block to most communication and understanding is self-thought. It's a wall.

There is too much static for any message to come through.

Exactly. Dance is consciousness made visible, as music is consciousness made audible. When I meet someone, what I am really doing is listening to their vibration. Words can be so confusing because often what people are saying is not what they really mean, so you have to listen behind the words.

How do you coach the dancers to "get out of the way"?

It's not an easy thing to do. So much of present-day training is focused on showing yourself. Ideas are always larger than personalities. For example, an incredible dancer I worked with danced beautifully in rehearsal, just beautifully, but when she got to the stage it changed. I asked her, "It was so deep in rehearsal—what happened?" She told me, "I wanted them to like me." Her radiance and the clarity of her address had been diminished because of her desire to be appreciated. During that performance, the audience had not received her real gift.

Another aspect of what she was saying was, "I want to receive. I want to feel, I want something in return." It's a tremendous amount of work and effort to expend, and it is a natural thing to want to be appreciated. Nonetheless, the job is to serve the art regardless of how it feels or what you get back.

Do you like feedback from the dancers?

I like physical feedback. I like to see understanding. When we are beginning a new work, I avoid too many words.

Alonzo, do you believe that "one is born a dancer"?

Most of the times when people are talking about talent in dance, they are referring to a physical facility, but what is really required is a strong mind with a deep fascination with, and dedication to, the art. There are certainly dancers who seem to be "born" to it, but there are other dancers who early in their training have a lot of difficulty, and years later they are amazing dancers. Does it mean that when they were struggling, they were untalented? Of course not. But what they had inside of them carving out their idea was an indomitable will. I think we carve out what we really want with perseverance and determination. Those who maintain that ravenous zeal and inner yearning are always the ones who achieve in dance. I'm not talking about fame or recognition, but the true experience of the art. More depends on willpower than even brain power.

Can you address the aspects of fame and celebrity?

When someone seeks fame, what they really want is omnipresence. When a person aches for power through money, position, status, the true craving is omnipotence, and the insatiable quest for knowledge is really the search for omniscience. All these things are our birthright, but we are following false signposts looking for home. It is within.

What we are taught to honor is celebrity, and what we are taught to trust is what makes lots of money. How then can an artist be respected or understood when people don't realize that they too are some kind of artist? It is what we are meant to be if we live full and authentic lives.

What are your thoughts about the future of dance? Are you concerned about it?

No. Dance is part of our makeup. The principle expression of life is movement. Everything is in motion. We live in a vibratory creation. Everything that exists is humming together at different rates of vibration. Neutrons and electrons are dancing together. Sound and movement are inextricably linked and from their union and cause in the Big Bang. In world cycles, there are times of ignorance and times of illumination; trends rise and fall, but dance will never disappear. Art cannot die anymore than electricity can die. We may be ignorant of it, but it is there nonetheless. It is a knowledge. It is by the art within us that things are made.

6

Danny Grossman

"He is a mime artist with the physicality of a football player and the gestural repertoire of an actor with great emotional depth. But his dances don't deal with dance. Rather, they are personal and emotional stories that align themselves with an overriding universal story."

—————**Daryl Jung,** *Now* **Magazine**

Danny Grossman in *Curious Schools of Theatrical Dancing*. Copyright *Andrew Oxenham. Courtesy of the Danny Grossman Dance Company.*

The founder and artistic director of the Danny Grossman Dance Company, based in Toronto, Canada, for over two decades, Grossman was a former virtuoso dancer with the Paul Taylor Dance Company (dancing under the professional name of Daniel Williams). He grew up amid the churning political climate of San Francisco during the McCarthy era and the Peace Movement. His father was a labor and civil rights lawyer who defended the Native Americans during the occupation of Alcatraz. His mother was one of the founders of the *Women for Peace* movement, a group working for the abolishment of nuclear weapons. They made sure that Grossman as a young child and teenager was exposed to the social injustices of the time, and took him at age ten to march in his first picket line. Both parents were threatened with subpoenas from the House Committee on Un-American Activities because of their political involvement during the Cold War. Those early years would help to fashion not only Grossman's political views but his choreography. The themes of man's inhumanity towards man, the evils of war, racism, and sexual liberation appear as a stamp in his works.

Endangered Species was dedicated to "all people in the world who work for international disarmament and world peace" and was inspired by Goya's etchings "The Disasters of War." *Species* is a compelling and provocative work that Grossman has taught to both young and mature dancers. *Nobody's Business,* set to the ragtime music of Jelly Roll Morton and Joe Turner, is a humorous parody of sexual mores that depicts Grossman's sexual liberation. He told me that *Nobody's Business* was joyous to make and dance, and that it announced that "This is what I am sexually, and if women want to lick the men, they can do it; and if men want to be femmes, it ain't nobody's business what we do."

The aesthetic response must contain elements of magic, for the mysteries that surround, block, and propagate creative impulses cannot always be known and hence named. For Grossman, that connection requires an inner journey much like the spiritual healers of other cultures who travel to other dimensions to retrieve their visions. *Visionary Realm* explores his personal journey into the shamanic realms of consciousness. These inner excursions are integral to his choreography, and they play pivotal roles in both his professional work and his personal evolution."All of my dances are journeys," he told me.

> The solos are personal journeys confronting death and the group works are societal journeys. I have gone to all of these realms like a shaman both physically and personally and come back to make dances for the people. Every time I do a dark psychological work, I journey to the underworld and come back with a new vision.

Grossman is willing to navigate his inner terrain, even when that navigation is painful.When he was brutally assaulted on tour in Paris, he used that experience in his dance *Ces Plaisirs*.The piece delves into the underworld of predatory sex and the emptiness of sex when it is based on sexual adventure without love. He told me that it was about "transcending my own life step by step." Sexuality is a frequent theme in his choreography, and he is not afraid to show "sex as sex and not as an arabesque." *Higher* is an acrobatic and highly charged sexual duet in which Grossman, his female partner, a ladder, and two chairs share the stage, honoring women and sexuality.

His choreography contains sexual, theological, and controversial themes, and those ideas provide for rich and powerful theatrical experiences. However, his choreography doesn't contain these subjects for shock value or titillation. Grossman's passion and commitment to social awareness led him to make dances that align with his personal philosophical questions about life, death, transformation, and interpersonal relationships.

Often he uses his talents as teacher, humorist, dancer, and choreographer to present the full range of human experiences in an effort to move audiences out of their malaise. Because of the subject matter of the work, audiences are frequently jolted into discussion. The themes of his dances have ignited controversy. During one performance at a high school, the Danny Grossman Dance Company was escorted out of the theatre midway during the production of *National Spirit*, a satire on American patriotism.

Grossman was a cheerleader in high school and studied modern dance with Gloria Unti, his teacher in San Francisco. Unti, like Paul Taylor, was wise enough to use Grossman's unique athletic physicality in the choreography without trying to change his unclassical stature.

In 1963, his world changed when he attended a summer school session at Connecticut College. At a party, his impromptu dancing caught the eye of Paul Taylor, who invited him to take classes with his company in New York City. A few months later, Grossman was a company member and remained with the Paul Taylor Dance Company for ten years. During those years, he cut his teeth in some of Taylor's most enduring works, including the haunting *Big Bertha* (where he premiered Taylor's lead role when Taylor was injured) and the exquisite *Aureole*. After Taylor's tutelage, he left the company a seasoned performer.

In 1973, he joined the faculty at York University in Toronto and performed with the Toronto Dance Theatre as guest artist and guest choreographer. In 1975, he decided to form his own dance company, where he continues to teach, choreograph, and educate the community about the powers of dance and dancemaking.

Grossman has taught master classes at the Juilliard School of Music and Drama, Brown University, Simon Fraser University, the Performing Arts Workshop, the Paul Taylor Studio, the Harlem Dance Foundation, and Ryerson York University. He received Canada's prestigious Jean A. Chalmers Award for choreographic distinction in 1978. A decade later, he earned Canada's Dora Mavor Moore Award for his solo work *Memento Mori*. He has been honored by the Dance Legacy Institute and received a commission by them to create two repertory études for educators and dance students.

As guest artist, he has appeared with Rudolf Nureyev in *Nureyev and Friends* at the Coliseum Theater in London, at Jacob's Pillow in Norman Walker's *Celestial Circus,* and the National Ballet of Canada's gala *A Diamond Night at the Ballet.*

Danny Grossman and Company have toured in seventeen countries and in every province and territory in Canada. His choreography has been performed by numerous companies, including the Paris Opera Ballet, the National Ballet of Canada, and Lés Grand

Ballets Canadiens. Various children's dance companies, for example, DancEast and Canadian Children's Dance Theatre, include his
choreography as part of their permanent repertoire.

When I spoke with Grossman, I was pleased that he was not
only articulate about the mysteries of dancemaking but that he was
anxious to demystify the psychological and spiritual implications
that appear in his works, a subject that often choreographers shun.

Whom do you consider mentors in your life, Danny?

My parents were my first mentors. I was influenced by my parents'
support of the underdog. I admired their courageous political atti-
tudes of socialism in the McCarthy age. They were subpoenaed because of their left-wing beliefs and their opposition to war and racism.
I was also influenced by their amazing collection of music and art.

Paul Taylor was definitely a mentor, but there were other influences since my work is so different from his. I was tremendously influenced by dancing in his work and "living it" from the inside. I had
an unclassical body and a circus physicality, and Paul used it to
death in the sense that I trained my body to do more than it ever
could by dancing his movements, and in that sense, he really was a
mentor. In terms of style, my work has been influenced by Charlie
Chaplin and Ray Charles. I was influenced by the physicality of dance.
I was born to dance.

What was it like for you growing up in San Francisco during the 1960s, experiencing your parents political activities with them?

Their environment of friends, who were united in what they believed in order to create a better world, made it very interesting for a
child. I met all sorts of people who were very eccentric.The parties
we attended were always multigenerational, and the picnics we would
go to were usually to raise money for a cause. There was always a
mixture of kids, grandparents, folk singers, and folk art around. It was
a very happy existence for me. I had to go back to those early influences in my own choreography when I left Paul, and my work stems
from those early years.

Did you have any inclinations for dancing when you were a child?

I loved to dance, but I didn't know that you could make a living as a dancer and that anyone would ever like you if you were a dancer.

Do you believe that "one is born a dancer"?

I have seen wonderful dancers from all over the world who didn't make a profession of it. You always see them; they take over the dance floor and everyone backs up. It's not *just* having a profession—it must be a physical need. They have to do it.

I used to go out late after my performances and try to see these dancers when I was on tour. It's a gift, and often I would meet them and they would talk to me and they "knew." They knew I was a younger dancer and that I was watching them to learn from them. But it wasn't just the dancers I loved—it wasn't elitist like that—it was a force, and people have it throughout the world who were never officially "dancers."

Who were your modern-dance influences?

Gloria Unti was an early influence, and that influence continued in my training with Gertrude Shurr, May O'Donnell, Wishmary Hunt, and Don Farnworth in New York City. Unti put me in her work and allowed me to be creative in it. She selected the movements that I could do well and made a work of art with them, instead of forcing me to do something I wasn't meant to do. All of my teachers allowed me to believe that I could dance. They were encouraging to me, and they never took away my confidence. They empowered my will to dance.

Can you tell me more about the moment that Paul Taylor discovered you at a party?

I saw him come into the room, and I did every dance step that I did as a kid, because I was an improviser. There was always a period when the group would back up and I would have to dance with my partner. We were on the floor, under a limbo pole. It was absolute modern dance improvisation without any formula. The form was the song playing on the record player and the ritual. He asked me to take class, and a few months later I was in the company.

Danny Grossman as a teenager in Gloria Unti's studio. *Copyright 1963 by Phiz Mezey. Courtesy of the Danny Grossman Dance Company.*

When you were a young dancer in the Taylor Company, was there room for you to express yourself, even though it was his choreography? Did he allow for that freedom?

Yes. His work ran the gamut from narrative to the poetic to the intensely macabre, and I had all of that in my personality. *Aureole* was so beautiful and lyrical. When I was relaxed as a child, I would listen to Billie Holiday and cry like a baby one day and be happy like a lark the next day because I loved life. I was born to be in some of Paul's works.

Tell me about the first piece you ever performed with the company? What was that experience like for you?

It was a piece called *Party Mix.* Opening night, I was terrified. I shook through the whole thing, just as I did when I danced with Margy Jenkins at Roosevelt Junior High School. Something happened and I just kept dancing, and I was able to dance every step, and my jumps were higher than ever before. My part was certainly built for me because I had a springy and easy jump like a slinky. I could stop in the air for the moment, and I felt great. That dance hit my spirit, and it was fast as hell. I was a slow learner though, and I had to stand behind everyone, because if I was in front, or if I was feeling pressured, I was insecure.

Did Taylor's work come easily for you?

No. I was scared on the stage at first. I was scared to death and paranoid, but often by the third performance, I would think, "Why was I paranoid? I feel so at home." I grew as a performer quickly, but I was with Paul for ten years. I did lead an emotional and even a spiritual life, and dancing his work I learned how to rid myself of my demons as a performer and find ecstasy.

In the beginning of your career, you say you were scared. As you became more comfortable and more secure in the work, how did your performances change?

Out of fear comes a sense of ecstasy that leads to exaltation and a sense of peace or calm. During the best moments of performing, I found that.

When did the fear of performing leave you?

We danced three or four pieces a night, and usually by the last dance, the fear was gone. It often happened when you were so fatigued on tour, and then you were untouchable.

That must be a wonderful feeling to be able to surrender yourself to the dance like that—or is it terrifying?

No, it is like a bird in the wind. It's inevitable. In a piece like *Big Bertha*, the dramatic horror builds to a horrendous conclusion, utterly unintellectually mapped out. As you get older, you can map it out because you have lived those emotions both onstage and in your life. You can recall them, you remember where they came from, and you journey to that unconscious realm. Now I am able to recall the narrative and stay cool. You can summon it up just before, and you may even go into a state where you may cry when you are done, but then it is gone. You are finally relaxed and aren't afraid, and you know that the audience isn't there to judge you. All of your fears really come from that, and all of a sudden you don't feel those fears anymore.

Can you tell me about your relationships with the other dancers in the company during the early years?

I had a wonderful friend, Carolyn Adams. We had a wonderful partnership with Paul. We loved each other onstage, and the audience could see that. We did all the lines of Paul's movement. We were both musical, and he choose beautiful music. Afterwards, we were very critical and supportive, and not just in technical ways. The spirituality of the parts was the real heart of the matter. When I was dancing with Paul, I was analyzing my work with a brilliant woman who was an organic thinker and who was spiritual and artistic. I was lucky because I had a work of art to live in.

Did you have any rituals that you would engage in before you performed?

There may have been times when I have had good-luck charms. When someone stole one of my rings, I was relieved that nothing dreadful happened. I would go to the theatre hours before a performance and warm up because my body was so tight. Remember, I was thrown into dance after only a couple years of training and then thrown onstage. I needed much more for my body to feel pliable and secure. I was not a cool performer, and I went places when I danced.

What do you mean "you went places"?

I literally lost myself when I could. I went out there to go to that other plane where you are not conscious and there isn't any separation between you and the audience. An example of that was when I was dancing *Big Bertha,* a social satire that showed a very dark world. It is about an all-American family at a carnival. The family becomes controlled by the band machine called *Big Bertha.* The father rapes the daughter, the mother does a striptease, and ultimately the family breaks down. I premiered it, and I went into this very dark place that was in me onstage. I was in the piece dramatically right away.

Can you speak about the contrast in dancing the luminous work *Aureole*?

Aureole was made when Paul was still a young man. It is such a beautiful, simple, human-affirming piece, such simple but fine choreography. *Aureole* means light, and it was the other side of my personality. Right away, you have to be there spiritually, not warming up to be lovely in the last section. Ideally you are an angel from the beginning, and to get into that spell there is a lot of work to do. As you get older, you don't have to rev up for that one, just define what is right before you go on. You can call it up in a second. When you are young, you have to find that physically, without thinking; physically, you have to get in that spell or trance.

Can you speak about Paul Taylor's influence on you in terms of your own personal growth?

Paul let us into his life, and we became a family in a sense, and he facilitated our becoming ourselves. He was incredibly generous, and in many respects that was probably hurtful to him in some ways. He had a tremendous generosity for me to become me.

How did he encourage that growth?

Just by our worlds meeting. He trusted all of us who were strong-willed and would later move on. I think he was very accepting of us as people. He certainly gave us the opportunity to dance, but that is almost the smallest part of what I am saying. Everyone could say that we loved him. When you look at what each of us has gone on to do, well, he facilitated that process. We didn't know how long it would last, and the inevitable took over for all of us to follow our own charts.

I was living in this beautiful work because of him. I know the pain I must have been to him. I was spoiled and obnoxious. Somehow, we were uniquely drawn together at a crucial time. When I waved good-bye to Paul, I think there were too many years in which I wished my works would feel like his. But, of course, this was never meant to be.

It must have been very difficult for you to make the decision to leave the company.

It was almost impossible because I had put myself and my physicality so deeply in his work that I felt that I had created them.

What did dancing Paul's work give to you?

I think I gave to the work, but I also grew from it. It gave me something to live and breathe. It gave me a place to dance the lessons of my own life, as well as to learn what great dance has to teach about life. You have to eat a lot of great food and you have to live great work. Great work isn't necessarily the work of a famous person. There are lots of great works around. Some dancers didn't become famous, but they were deep artists who learned how to make fine work. An artist has to live; they live in the work and the work lives through them.

Do you know the term *temenos*, or sacred ground?

Ruth St. Denis supposedly never set foot on the stage without knowing that it was a sacred place. I heard that when I was young, but thank God I didn't know what it meant then or it would have scared the hell out of me. I never would have gone on. You realize that potential, since the stage is like a cathedral. It's a wonderful place for all sorts of reality. You can show the worst demons or the most beautiful things. I think it is also a very truthful place, and yet it can also be a mean and sarcastic place. It is also used for great humanitarian beliefs, a belief in the human spirit, and the belief that the human spirit is grand.

Danny, your choreography reflects and explores many of the universal social and political ills in the world. Can you speak more about those components and why they are important to you?

I come from parents with great depth who have pioneering and courageous spirits. So did many of the dance pioneers. Their work was so specific; they were primal, they were clear, they were human, they were deep. They weren't confused; they weren't making dances with every image just thrown out onstage. They weren't artists who were victims of their own wild cacophony of ideas and emotions. Their work was so carved and etched and simple. That is where I come from. I have made some frightening and happy and playful dances to the best of my ability within that domain.

Has physical pain ever been a teacher to you in your career?

When I improvised that night at the party when Paul was there, I could barely walk the next day. All the years when I worked with him, when he was choreographing and I so wanted to give my all, the next day I would have so many sores on my knees that I couldn't duplicate the turns. I was willing to go into those spells of daring even though I knew I wouldn't be able to walk the next day. Then, you know, with adrenaline the pain would be gone. I would take a bath for an hour when I got home, and in the morning take another bath, and it all started again. I had great optimism. If I had to, I would go into the studio for an hour and a half to stretch, and before I knew it, I was back to square one. But by the end of the day, I wouldn't be able to walk again. I was young.

Was there any difference for you when you would choreograph your own work?

No one in their right mind would create some of the dances I have made. I had to go into those other dramatic states where you don't feel the pain.

Have you ever injured yourself while you were performing?

In 1991, I choreographed *Rite Time,* an ecstatic mating ritual with a limbo pole, set to the music of Ray Charles during his golden years. At the climax of the dance, the tribe elevates the dancing demon or wise man (myself) vertically on the pole. At the point of personal elevation as a performer, I started to experience physical deterioration. I had a simple ecstatic jump on one leg, and then "rip," I felt my calf muscle tear. Thank God, I was near the point where I would be carried around for the rest of the piece. I gripped my calf muscle tightly and did the best I could. I told the cast not to walk forward for the bows since I couldn't walk. When I recovered, I changed the jumps to the other leg. At the same point in the piece, the other calf muscle ripped. I said to myself, "OK, I get it now."

Let's talk about your first work, *Higher.*

Higher was choreographed in 1975; and it's a sexual duet for a man and woman and is set to the music of Ray Charles. It was designed like the *Kama Sutra,* and the dancers slide through a ladder onstage. The implications are wonderful. I took all the knowledge and the desire to make a dance from my many years with Paul.

Some of my friends thought it was sexist, and others thought it was physically outrageous. But if you look closely at the movements, sometimes the woman is on top, and sometimes he is on top. It's really about the battle of the sexes. The piece was about sexual relationships in relation to the spirit and the spirituality of sex. You know, I show sex as sex and not as an arabesque. I design it so the audience knows exactly what is going on and it is clear. To make a work like that, whatever your sexuality, you have to love women and you have to love sexuality. I used to take a shot of brandy so that I was fearless of the perilous feats on stage.

Your first solo was *Curious Schools of Theatrical Dancing,* made in 1977. Can you tell me what the process was like in making that piece?

Curious was titled after a book from 1716 by Lambranzi, which illustrated theatrical dances of the period. It is a paranoid dance to the death and tells the story of a crippled harlequin set to music by Francois Couperon. I created the dance by digging deep physically and emotionally. It's really in the muscles; it is very visceral. You have to get to that state where that comes out, not what you think you have to choreograph. A more advanced personal journey came to me when I made that piece.

How did you work on it? Did you work alone or with other dancers?

When you make a solo for yourself, it's not a good idea to set it on someone else. At some point, it's better to get another dancer and teach them so you can watch it and get a sense of the design, and then kick them out of the room, otherwise it becomes their dance.

What did it feel like for you to perform that solo?

The absolute paranoia of looking at the audience was draining, and if I relaxed in this dance, it would not be a dance to the death. I dreaded dancing *Curious* more than anything else in the repertoire, because it is terrifying and you are running the entire time. In the beginning, I would look at the audience with the lights blinding me and I would say, "What are you looking at?" At the end, I ignored the audience and would reach straight to God. I could barely move and I was absolutely crippled. Anyone who dances this piece feels queasy all day. Every night that I danced it, I went to that place where I created it, where I had been in my earlier life—running and hiding as a homosexual or feeling the political persecution of my parents. For the ten years that I performed that piece, I had to keep going to that place.

Even after performing it for so many years, you still weren't able to remove the emotional content?

You can with certain dances, but with this one, it doesn't work. By the time I stopped dancing it, I had figured out how to use very little extra energy. When you are a mature performer, you just click it on and the rest is easy, but by then, you can't physically perform it as easily.

Did the creation of that dance help you personally?

Yes. It was a tremendous purge.What happens often is that a

work of art is created that is more evolved spiritually then when you created it.

It's fascinating to me that the spiritual component would be in place but that it would take years for you to understand that growth.

That's why it is important that the dance be done and done and done. It's not that the overall design isn't there from the beginning, but you don't quite know what you have until you start directing the drama and realize where it came from in your own life. This happens to all of my work that doesn't abort. Sometimes, you have people on the outside who tell you things, and they are right, but there are still things to discover from the inside, and the dance just grows and grows.

I remember that you told me that you thought you were a "healthier person" with each dance that you made. That statement is very

Danny Grossman. *Copyright Cylla von Tiedemann. Courtesy of the Danny Grossman Dance Company.*

revealing. When you made *Ces Plaisirs,* did it stem from the beating in Paris, or were you looking at the sexual roles that people play?

I loved Collette's book *The Pure and the Impure,* and the way she not only lived some of these sexual situations but stood away from them and wrote about them as her own life evolved. The very time I was reading this book, I was beaten up in Paris outside a gay bar. I was kicked and kicked. I remember that she wrote about one lonely guy who finds the man of his dreams and he takes him home, and the man takes off his clothes and he is actually a woman. The poor guy kills himself. I don't have that in my story, but I replaced him with a figure who is beat up. It's an impeccably clinical piece, like looking in a window without any emotion, but it's devastatingly sad. The dance is about myself, transcending my own life, step by step.

***Ces Plaisirs* makes an important commentary on sex and sexual identification and, most importantly, the sexual games that men and women play.**

Yes. In 1985, when I made the work, I set it in a whorehouse using Colette's characters: prostitutes, predators, and a voyeur. It deals with sexual perversion and voyeurism, but it is more than that; it is a journey of awakening that comes after the suppression of sexuality is released. It is also a dance about looking for sex without love, and it's very tragic.

Three female prostitutes are exploited by male predators, and one is a woman who appears as a man. Once the women are no longer playing sexual games they become friends, but the voyeur and the predator's lack of real human companionship is the loneliest aspect of the piece. When the voyeur crawls off the stage, he crawls off with his pants tied around his neck, so it looks as though he hanged himself. In certain dances, I have used my own life and my own politics. Sometimes I have even captured the ideology of a woman in my work. This was not a sexual piece; it was a spiritual piece.

You tackled the subject of homosexuality in *Nobody's Business.* Was that a difficult piece for you to create?

No, it was not a problem at all. I certainly could be secretive in my private life, but not onstage, which was odd. I would find humorous or dramatic ways to be specifically clear about that, like a movie. You know, an audience is willing to watch a movie about anything with a tight little script, if it's well acted and done with a little ingenuity. I made a joyous celebration before I was free to celebrate in public, or before I felt emotionally free. We took the piece everywhere, and even played it in small towns, because the dance is done with humor and with the music of Jelly Roll Morton and Joe Turner. We had the audience tittering.

Your work is very authentic and clear.

In *Nobody's Business,* I was out of the closet, dancing cheek to cheek with a man. It was tongue in cheek, which allowed me to get my message out in spite of the fact that society was not and is not that open about homosexuality. Heterosexual couples go about their lives publicly while others are ostracized from society. *Nobody's Business* was out of the closet physically before I was in my own life. I have lived with the same man since 1962.

Is he an artist as well?

He was. His name is Germain Pierce. He was a singer and a dancer, and he is also a fabulous cook and a very wise person. He has given me much of my music over the years and has really been the greatest mentor in my life. He is my life companion. In 1998, I made *Passion Symphony* for him, and although we are not in the dance, in it the male lovers guided by daemons are joined in sacred union.

Since much of your choreography has such a strong component of politics, have you ever had difficulties performing them in the sense of a cold audience response?

In most places, no, but once in Toronto at a children's theatre we performed *Nobody's Business,* and when we were done the teacher stood up and removed the class. They didn't have the chance to see the rest of the performance. The kids didn't have a problem with the subject matter, only the teacher did.

We also did *National Spirit* at an elementary school in Florida. It is a light-hearted send-up that I choreographed in 1976 to patriotic anthems and marches. It does imply, in a humorous way, that if you follow the leader, you can get killed. We were supposed to perform two shows, but the principal called us into her office and told us that she would not allow us to continue. She said, "It will take ten years to unteach what you have shown them." She even called the police. Over the years, my company has had a brush or two. Charlie Chaplin touched certain themes, too, and he tried to get his message across in a humorous way. What can you do? Be as clear as you can and just keep working.

I know that you often teach your choreography to children. Can you tell me more about your experiences, particularly about teaching works with religious themes?

Young people ages thirteen to seventeen have been in my work, and their parents usually are devastated when they watch the performance. They wonder how their child could know all of that? They do it with an innocence that makes it even more beautiful. They understand what it is about. They have performed sections of *Ecce Homo,* which is about religious ecstasy and sin and guilt on the almost nude body.

They have also performed *Triptych,* which is about abuse. It's about three desolate characters, and the work portrays physical abuse with political undercurrents. When I created it, I went into the studio with some old clothes—some dark and some bright. The characters in the dance peel off their clothing to reveal the brightness of their souls. It is a very spiritual piece. Both of these dances have been performed by children and adults. The children bring a beauty and a simplicity to it that is quite remarkable.

What happens when you go to the studio to work? Has your creative process evolved over the years?

In the beginning, I would try to find the movement, and now it comes from having a clear indication of what the dance is about. I have a group of artists who, after several years with me, know the repertoire. The more mature dancers are more in tune with my search, and the younger ones use their amazing intuitive physicality, so be-

Danny Grossman teaching in San Francisco at the Performing Arts Workshop. *Copyright Ed Buryn. Courtesy of the Danny Grossman Dance Company.*

tween the sensing of the elders and the physicality of the younger
ones, and myself, it is created. There is still that trust, and you have
to allow things to happen. You have to be looking.

What do you mean?

You have to be totally open so that you see things out of the cor-
ners of your eyes. As the dancers are experimenting in trying to
achieve what you want, you can say, "That was it!" when it appeared
that you were looking the other way. Now I work the palette that way.

**Can your work be danced by older dancers, given the physical
demands needed?**

Artists could dance my work *Triptych* when they are sixty years old. In my work I need many ages of humanity to give it depth—the young war horses who can navigate the whole repertoire, as well as the mature dancers who enrich the repertoire with the content of their lives. Many so-called nonprofessional dancers, children and adults, have been able to both receive and give to the work.

Do you find your dreams useful to you in your choreography?

I had a dream several years ago, and in it my parents were walking across a wooden, Golden Gate Bridge. They were both elderly, and I told them not to worry, that I would go ahead. On the other side, a wolf came down and grabbed me by the neck and pulled me down. Then I woke up. I was irritated that I woke up since I thought this was so real. This was my chance to get torn apart and come back wiser like the shaman, but I was afraid.

Some years after this dream, I made *Visionary Realm,* a dance about transformation. In the dance, the shaman, guided by animal spirits, transcends opposing forces of male and female and birth and death to journey to the solar realm (or the beginning), and returns to earth with a new sense of balance. The shaman has physical understanding of androgyny. That aspect related to my own life, being attracted to both male and female.

Do you have a spiritual practice, Danny?

There is a Buddhist poem that says that many of us run back and forth on one side while others cross over to transformation. I am interested in that process. Going to the studio and thinking about these things is a meditation. I have always been interested in reading books that deal with my own transformation to become a happier person.

Can you describe the philosophy of your work to me?

All of my dances are journeys. The solos are personal journeys confronting death, and the group works are societal journeys that confront destruction and the transformation process. They are always autobiographical, but they reflect the universal aspects. As an artist, like a shaman, I have gone to all of these realms, both physically and personally, and I've come back to make dances for people. There has always been a lot of sex in my work because my dances are quite primal. The connection between sexuality and life and death in my work is very obvious and clear. I believe that nothing in life, death, and beyond is connected without sex. It is an important part of the journey.

Your choreography echoes the depths of despair and the heights of ecstasy, and there isn't much middle ground. Does one come first?

They arrive almost at the same time. When I created *Nobody's Business,* it was joyous.The same year I choreographed *Endangered Species,* which is about the extermination of human beings. It was absolutely imperative in those early years that the depths of despair went with the highest ecstasy. You have to understand those two dimensions. It's the balance between them as well. I have dealt with the highs and the lows as a performer and as a creator in my own life and have achieved a balance.

Do you feel as if your work presently is taking you into a new direction?

Recently, I returned to the music of my childhood. I grew up hearing Paul Robeson, the great activist, actor, and singer, and I think at one point I sat on his knee as a kid. I chose spirituals he sang that I love, made drawings, and worked from an incident that happened to my father when he was a lawyer defending a black man unjustly accused of raping a white woman. My father was beaten by the authorities and almost killed, and the accused man was executed. I created *Hear the Lambs A Cryin'* in 1997 with great ease.

How do you think that dance can best be served by your work?

I want to use the company to present dance that is about humanity, dance that is clear, concise, daring, and universal and is not afraid of subject matter. I believe that art expresses values. My repertoire and the company reflect my personal values of equality, pacifism, honesty, courage, social responsibility, sympathy for the underdog, and a willingness to reveal the demons. I believe that dance should educate and transform the audience.

What is your vision for the future?

When I was in his company, I was in Paul Taylor's web. I learned in those confines. Then I came to Canada and started to spin a web of my own with my dancers. I thought I was alone, but the web was spun the minute I was born. I am part of a universal garden that has been growing the whole time.

Now, with my dancers, we came together organically because there was a need to do something, and a body of work was created. This work has nourished us as artists, and I hope we have nourished our community as well. The dancers are co-creators of the work; they share in the journey. They are the blood and memory of the work, and they pass it onto the next generation.

What are your thoughts about the future of dance?

I haven't a clue. The cutbacks do scare me, but after a point you don't worry about it. I am a director of a company, an incredibly fortunate company that has received tremendous support from the arts councils and audiences in Canada. It takes tenacity to survive. It is funny that at the point when we have the most to give, the funding is slipping away. What I can't do anymore is worry about it. It must be balanced against the odds. It's not that different from becoming an artist to beat the odds and survive.

In the late 1980s, I was on a beach in Vancouver. I saw a freighter sailing from the bay into the ocean. This reminded me of a trip to Asia that I took in 1960 when I sailed underneath the Golden Gate Bridge into the rough waters of the Pacific Ocean. I cried like a baby because I had come full circle and felt my life was over. I could remember the moments of joy, sadness, and calm. I had no idea in 1960 that any of this was going to happen to me and that I would have a calling in such a difficult profession and lead an inspired life. I realized that the freighter was not a metaphor that my life was over but a symbol of re-birth. I knew I would sail again. I feel that I have to stick to the life force. Most important to me is certain psychological and social trans-formations and to return to my true nature.

7

Michael Smuin

"Smuin is choreographic theater personified. . . . As a director he has few ballet peers . . . and as a choreographer pure and simple, even though he is rarely either, he dares with an imagination that runs happily from Maryinsky to Las Vegas."

————Clive Barnes, *On the Town. New York Post,* May 1980

When a dance is created, it should be a dance well worthy of record, a work by one who has looked at life and, most importantly, immersed oneself in that life. Michael Smuin is such an artist. A consummate craftsman, Smuin blends musicality and theatricality, capturing his audiences' attention whether he is making dances for the Broadway stage, opera productions, film, television specials, or for his own company in San Francisco, Smuin Ballets/SF.

He knows what makes for an evening of dazzling performance, and his dancing career has provided him with a rich palette to draw upon. With over 160 ballets, his choreographic scope is staggering, and he has a mantle full of awards in his living room to prove it.

Smuin has received the triumvirate of dance awards: a Tony Award, Drama Desk Award, and a Fred Astaire Award for his choreography for the Broadway musical *Anything Goes*. For decades of choreographic work, he has received five Emmy Awards, two Tony nominations (for *Sophisticated Ladies*), an Outer Circle Critics Award, the Montana Governor's Award for the Arts, and an award from *Dance Magazine*.

Smuin has worked with a virtual who's who in entertainment, and the short list includes Leonard Bernstein (for the production of *Candide* at the opening of the Kennedy Center), Gene Kelly, Shirley MacLaine, Bob Fosse, Dean Martin, Frank Sinatra, Maurice Chevalier, Jack Nicholson, Tony Bennett, Linda Ronstadt, Bobby McFerrin, Peggy Lee, Anthony Hopkins, Richard Gere, Anthony Quinn, Joel Grey, Angie Dickinson, Woody Allen, Gregory Hines, and Nicholas Cage.

Extending the boundaries of ballet vocabulary, he is able to take dance to its outer limits, frequently departing from the conventions of classical ballet vocabulary. Smuin makes his own unique comment but is careful not to usurp that vocabulary, for only one who has mastered the rules can break them. He has excelled partly because he possesses the uncanny ability not only to create what is needed for a particular dance genre but to understand those genres in depth.

When he was in his twenties and dancing with American Ballet Theatre with his wife, Paula Tracy (a gifted dancer and choreographer in her own right), they left their ballet careers to perform their

Michael Smuin in rehearsal for *A Song for Dead Warriors*. Copyright *James Armstrong*. *Reproduced by permission of the San Francisco Ballet.*

own cabaret act called "Michael and Paula." Working with the headliners of the time, they toured internationally and even appeared on the Ed Sullivan Show.

It is rare when a choreographer can easily step outside of the world of ballet to meet success, but Smuin defies the label "ballet choreographer." He has created a body of work for the San Francisco Ballet (where he reigned as artistic director for many years), American Ballet Theatre (where he was resident choreographer), and his present company. In addition, his choreography can be found in the repertoires of Dance Theatre of Harlem, the Washington Ballet, Pacific Northwest Ballet, Ballet West, Milwaukee Ballet, Ballet/Met, The Hartford Ballet, and Ballet Florida.

He brings to his choreography a keen education in theatre, with a capital T. He explained, "When I work on Broadway, I am the ballet guy. When I work in ballet, I am the Broadway guy."

Michael Smuin grew up in Missoula, Montana, and his first experience with dance occurred when he impulsively joined a group of Native American dancers during a ceremonial dance. Those impulses for dance led him to audition at the age of fourteen for William Christensen, who was then the director of the University of Utah's Dance Department. Christensen recognized the young man's talents and invited him to join the program even though Smuin hadn't even graduated from high school. Their association would prove fortuitous for both of them.

He left Utah in the late 1950s to join the San Francisco Ballet where Christensen's brother, Lew, sat at the helm. In five years, Smuin was appointed principal dancer, ballet master, and resident choreographer for the company. After serving in the United States Army, he left San Francisco Ballet to dance with American Ballet Theatre and stayed in New York for seven years. He returned to the Bay Area as artistic director for San Francisco Ballet when he was thirty-three years old, a position he held for twelve years until political infighting forced him to depart.

His years at San Francisco Ballet proved noteworthy. He was able to transform the company's image from a local dance company to a world class company. The company that previously performed in gymnasiums now danced at the White House, toured nationally, and garnered the respect they deserved. Three of his works were televised for the "Dance in America" series on PBS. He earned three of five Emmy Awards for those programs (*A Song for Dead Warriors, Romeo and Juliet*, and *The Tempest*). He received the other two Emmys as director/choreographer on "Voice/Dance" with Bobby McFerrin and "Canciones de Mi Padre" with Linda Ronstadt.

Smuin's innovations brought a new audience to San Francisco Ballet, fans who appreciated his out-of-the-ordinary work. He brought live buffalo onstage, set dances to the Beatles, and revitalized what audiences notions were of the ballet. He told me, "People accuse me of going "too far." But I think I didn't go far enough!"

Even though his ideas did not always curry favor with the critics, he had legions of fans. When his ballet *A Song for Dead Warriors* (based on the life of Indian rights activist Richard Oakes) was performed, he received a note that validated his vision and contribution. The note read: "I am very proud to see the songs, dances, costumes, sacred symbols, the inner feelings, and the great sense of beauty represented by your company with such great power. You create and perform all your beautiful dances from the heart."

Another admirer, Linda Ronstadt, used to fly to his performances just to see his ballets. She explained:

> Michael has the most amazing nerve. He always pushes for that extra thrill. Ballet should make you cry, scream, and gnash your teeth. People mistakenly think that you are supposed to fall asleep in ballet, and if it wakes you up, it's not elite enough. But Michael's work doesn't follow the rules; he shows you something about yourself. His work makes you realize certain feelings, and you can see the parts that are tender. He has a sharp stick for that.

Those poetic sensibilities were evident in his own career as a dancer. When he was with American Ballet Theatre he danced leading roles in *Billy the Kid, Fancy Free, Lés Patineurs*, and *Petrouchka*. Although he received great reviews, no one knew that he suffered from stage fright and often became physically ill before his performances.

The years he spent with American Ballet Theatre were particularly fruitful for his budding choreographic career in the 1960s. He made *The Catherine Wheel, Gertenfest, The Eternal Idol,* and *Pulcinella Variations.* When he set the ballet *Schubertiade,* Mr. Balanchine took notice. Backstage, he told him, "You used the music in the right way. Right way to use Schubert. Good boy."

Smuin was in New York when it was glistening with talent and was fortunate enough to be surrounded by the best minds in dance, music, and theatre. He told me:

> I was in Ballet Theatre when "everybody" was there.
> I worked with everyone with the exception of Martha
> Graham. Aaron Copland, Duke Ellington, Morton
> Gould—all of the great artists. I just soaked it up. I would
> sit and talk with them and learn so much. They would tell
> me to "read this book" or "go see this exhibition." It was
> a fabulous education.

During the time he was in New York, he flirted with the possibility of pursuing a film career and often sought out vintage films as sources of inspiration for his roles. Many years later (in 1983) he worked with Francis Ford Coppola to create *Romanze,* a ballet on film shown in tandem with a dance performance. It's an elegant and sensual ballet exploring the sexual longings of a Victorian woman, inspired by Smuin's discovery of a woman's diary from that era.

He has worked as a film choreographer on *Rumble Fish, Cotton Club, Dracula, The Fantasticks, A Walk in the Clouds, Wolf, Golden Gate, Corridos, The Joy Luck Club, Angie, Fletch,* and *Return of the Jedi.* Several years ago, Smuin attended the Sundance Film Institute's Writers' and Directors' Lab to explore his ideas for a film called *Born in a Trunk.*

Smuin spoke to me on his birthday at his home in San Francisco. We talked at length, and during our meeting he showed me his enormous collection of choreographic notebooks meticulously organized with his handwritten notes, musical scores, photographs, and sketches. He also showed me the beautiful Japanese garden in his backyard and the sculptures he creates to "unwind."

After the interview, his wife, Paula, graciously let me peruse the scrapbooks she has collected over the years, laden with photos and clippings from their careers.

Michael, I would like to know more about your process of creating a ballet. Can you take me through the stages?

It depends on what type of piece it is, but for me it's almost always the music. Sometimes you have an idea, but you can't find the music. For example, the idea for the ballet *Hearts* started with the movie *Les Enfants de Paradise*. I listened to hundreds of French composers and I couldn't find what I needed, so someone suggested Edith Piaf's music. It was perfect for this ballet.

I have this wonderful collection of mambo music that I have accumulated through the years. I kept thinking, "How can I use this?" Then I thought of *Frankie and Johnny* and set it in some seedy bar in Havana in the 1950s.

Do your ideas come to you very quickly?

No. After I have an idea, the process in the studio is very quick, but it is very difficult to think it completely through. We used the music of Mozart for *Cyrano* because it's a ballet about words; it's about poetry. It's not all that visual—even the sword fights are words—so you need to find metaphors to show those words.

How important is it to you if the audiences get it or not?

Its very important to me if the audience gets it. I could care less whether the critics get it or not, because most of them don't. But its very important to me that the audience responds even though they may not intellectually know what is happening, but emotionally it happens. That's really my job.

How important is it to you to make political work? I am thinking specifically about *A Song for Dead Warriors*. Where did you get the idea for that ballet?

That ballet crept up on me. When Richard Oakes took over Alcatraz with a Native American woman (who was actually the leader), it was front-page news in the Bay Area for almost a year. I thought maybe there was a ballet in the story. Oakes was badly beaten in a bar-room fight, and he spent three weeks in a coma. When he woke up, he told his wife about his dreams, which were later published. I thought that his dreams were very balletic. But I wasn't trying to make a statement about the Indian situation in this country; it was just that his particular story was fascinating to me, especially his dreams.

Do you discuss your ideas with anyone, or do you find it helpful to keep them close to you?

I speak to the lighting designer and the costume designer and anybody who is creatively involved. I talk to them a lot, and I also talk to the dancers, and they will often come up with terrific ideas.

Do you welcome input from the dancers? I know some choreographers don't like to engage the dancers in their creative process.

I love it. I think it is great, and it makes my job so much easier when someone comes up with a good idea. Balanchine loved it, and when someone came to rehearsal with a great idea, he would often use the steps.

Tell me more about your experiences with Mr. Balanchine.

I never had that much opportunity to deal with him. He came to San Francisco Ballet a few times. He saw one of my ballets called *Schubertiad* and came backstage and told me, "Very good ballet, you used the music the right way. Right way to use Schubert. Good boy. Nice, dear."

Considering how young you were when you made that piece, that was an encouraging comment from a master.

Yes. When I was in Ballet Theatre, he told Patty Wilde that he thought I really "had something." He came to the theatre a few times to work on *Theme and Variations.* I happened to be in the corps de ballet then, and I watched him work. He never sat down, he stood up the whole time during the rehearsal. I worked more with Jerry Robbins than Balanchine because Jerry was around Ballet Theatre more. I did bigger roles in *Fancy Free, Interplay, Noce's,* yet I always wanted to do *Afternoon of a Faun.*

What was it like to work with Mr. Robbins?

He was very difficult. He was mean, but great.

Wasn't he a choreographer who didn't like you to change any of the steps?

Yes. You had to do it exactly. There is a whole type of modus operandi when he did a ballet, and it changed with the work and the problems that he had that fell within the work. But there was nobody better than Jerry Robbins.

In your early training as a dancer, you had the chance to use your knowledge of music and drink up the atmosphere with some of the most compelling artists of that time. What was that experience like for you?

I went to all of the exhibitions of all the painters. I really soaked it up. I happened to be in Ballet Theatre at the time when everybody was there. I worked with every major choreographer, major designer, and major composer with the exception of Martha Graham. Aaron Copland was there, Morton Gould, Duke Ellington, Oliver Smith . . . all of the really great artists were there.

You could sit and talk to them and you could learn. They often would tell me to "read this book" or "see this exhibition" or go see a particular movie. As a choreographer, I think I learned more about the process of putting things together, not only from other choreographers but from filmmakers. Buster Keaton, Charlie Chaplin, those people put together wonderful stories without the aid of words. I learned choreography from their films.

It's fascinating to me that you not only saw film as an inspiration for your dancing but you recognized the parallels to dancemaking.

Choreography is like architecture, and architecture is like movies,

Michael Smuin in *Ribbon Dance* from *The Nutcracker*. Photographer *unknown*. *Reproduced by permission of the San Francisco Ballet.*

and it's also like storyboarding. I think I learned so much from people like Buster Keaton and Charlie Chaplin and the great German film-makers—Fritz Lang, Max Reinhardt, Leni Riefenstahl—and the French filmmakers—Jean Cocteau, Truffault, and also Fellini and Kuirosowa. When you watch their movies, they are such lessons in choreography, because all you have to do is look at what they have done and add steps to it and put music to it.

Was there a particular work you danced that you really loved and felt a bond with physically and emotionally? A piece that felt incredible when you were performing it?

Every time I did *Fancy Free,* I felt that the part was made for me. Even when I was sick or had a fever and felt like hell, the music would start and I was instantly transformed. It was always fun to do, but it was exhausting to dance. *Billy the Kid* was also one of those ballets that you could sink your teeth into. I don't think that the audiences ever really dug *Billy the Kid* the way they dug *Fancy. Fancy* was much more of a personal work. It was great fun to dance, but I don't think that the audience was ever completely turned on by *Billy.*

When you were dancing, did you ever feel as if you were in a more heightened state when you were performing? Can you describe it?

Well, there is always a high onstage, sure. For example, when Enrique Martinez wanted me to do *Dr. Coppelia,* I went to rehearsal and I just didn't have a feel for it. Then I happened to attend a Charlie Chaplin film festival and I got my ideas for that character from his films. I had been working on the part, and I added a whole bunch of vaudevillian gags to the part. You know, when I was onstage and felt the laughs from the audience, it was a kick, letting the people laugh with you.

Can you tell me more about the mental preparation that you would do?

Well, I was always terrified before I danced. I had stage fright like you can't believe. I had stage fright to the point where I would actually throw up before I would go on. Sometimes on opening night when I was dancing a very important role and I was doing difficult steps, I would say to myself, "After this performance, this is it." But once I got from here to there, I was perfectly comfortable. It was just so difficult getting out there.

Do you know what the fear was?

I have no idea, but my knees would be weak and I would feel sick and dizzy. You know, I always envied the dancers who could put their makeup on and go out onstage calmly. For them, it was like they were performing in their living rooms. But I always suffered before I got on.

Was your fear in any relation to the difficulty of the role?

You know, I really don't know. I was technically a very strong dancer. I was a virtuoso dancer; I could do all that stuff. I don't think it was that I thought that I couldn't do the steps.

Were you afraid you would forget the steps?

No, maybe. But it was just getting onstage in front of people, and, of course, you can't see; it's dark out there.

Would it be pleasurable for you once you began to dance?

Oh, yeah, once I got onstage I was at home. Just getting there was awful. Even today when I know I have to make a curtain speech or a spiel of some sort, I get very nervous. For my mother's birthday party, recently, I was in a state, and I had to tell my brother to pour me a bourbon.

Paul Taylor told me that he didn't enjoy performing either.

I did have a good time once I got out there. Most of my roles were show-off roles—the Green Boy in *Lés Patineurs,* the First Sailor in *Fancy*—it was a show-off kind of thing, and the audiences immediately took to it, so you felt like you were in a friendly atmosphere.

I would assume that during the next evening performance, your fears would subside and you were OK?

No, I was terrified again, terrified, really scared. My mouth would be so dry no matter know much water I drank. My knees would be so weak, and I would always feel sick.

Did you ever have a particular ritual that would help you thorough?

I would knock on wood. I *had* to find wood. It couldn't be synthetic and it couldn't be Formica. Sometimes backstage it's hard to find wood since everything is steel or plastic or Formica.

You danced Bill Christensen's ballet that he made especially for you, called *Dionysus,* at the University of Utah when you were a teenager. Wasn't that your first starring role?

Yes, it probably was. I have pictures of it with me in a little Greek tunic, and I have olive leaves on my head. You know, it was probably a terrible ballet, but I do remember it.

Was Bill your mentor at that time?

Probably. Yet the heroes I had were either writers or filmmakers or poets; they were never dancers or choreographers or actors. It was the film directors who I admired. I would think, "How did John Ford make this great western?"

They were so wonderful. I am talking about his films where frame after frame would go by with no dialogue, and yet you knew exactly what the story was. I thought this was great. I consider these guys almost like choreographers.

Watching so many films must have been great training for your eyes.

It was, because in these films, they weren't just about atmosphere. It was not just cowboys riding across the range. In all of these films, you see pictures that tell the story to you. You could look at the film for twelve minutes and there wouldn't be one word of dialogue. That always impressed me.

Film is a very similar art form to dance if you consider the importance of timing, lighting, costumes, and the movement in the story.

Yes. John Ford was great. I know people pooh-pooh him now, but, damn, that man could make good films. They still hold up. When there is a John Ford movie on TV now, for me everything stops. He was a great teacher for me.

How is choreographing for film different for you from choreographing for the stage?

Film is one eye. The camera is one eye. On the stage, it's all over the place; you can look wherever you want. If something fascinates you over there, that is where you look. With the camera, the director says, "Now, you are going to see *this*." You can also change the size of what you are looking for in film. It's less so for television because if you go too far away, dancers become this big and they become very uninteresting and they move very slowly, even when they are moving, very, very fast. They move slowly. The bigger the image, the faster they move.

Michael Smuin and Gene Kelly. *Photographer unknown.* Reproduced by permission of the San Francisco Ballet.

Do the challenges in working in film make it more difficult for your work as a choreographer?

No. You are so free. You can put the camera anywhere. I worked on a movie with Martin Short called *Best Wish*. In one scene, Kathleen Turner plays a witch who puts him in a trance and he becomes a mad Baryshnikov. But Short doesn't dance at all. However, in film you can do anything. I have him sliding down the banister with one foot in arabesque. I have him spinning forever because he is on a turntable. He lifts Turner by the foot with one hand and then she lifts him in the same way. It is all done with wires. It's great fun; you can't do that onstage. If you can't do it physically, you can use computers. You can do some magic on the stage but not like you can do in film.

When you worked with George Lucas, did you use computer-generated work?

Two of the characters were computer-generated, and there were two puppets, and the rest of the characters were real people. I did the blue screen for that. I also used the dancers from my company for *Return of the Jedi*. It was a very interesting experience because he was directing the movie himself.

Do you want to incorporate more film into your work? Is that the direction you want to continue to pursue?

I would have—I think I am too old to do that now. I think it's something you have to start when you are very young. The films I have worked on have been great experiences for me. For example, in *Dracula* and *Rumblefish*, Francis [Ford Coppola] let me do the scenes the way I wanted, so it was great.

Did you ever consider becoming a filmmaker?

There was a time in my life when I was dancing with Ballet Theatre when I really wanted to go to film school. I wanted to quit dancing and go to film school. Paula was dancing at that time, and she has her own career going and I would bring it up once in a while. I always felt that maybe I should have done that.

I think I would have made different types of films because of my dance background. I would have been the strange one in the film industry. My background is so bizarre and my ballets are different from other choreographers from my generation. You know, the real tragedy was Bob Fosse. He was turning out to be perhaps one of the great filmmakers of all time. *Cabaret* is almost perfect. If he had lived, who knows what he could have done?

Do you have a preference in terms of working in film or on Broadway?

I much rather do film since I believe that film is really the medium of our day. Live theater is one thing, but film brings the best people together: writers, composers, designers, and specialists of all sorts. I believe that the best creative minds working today are in film.

Do you have more artistic freedom in film?

I don't think it gives you much artistic freedom at all. I mean even George Lucas has his problems. When he told me about what he wants to do and that he has problems with things getting approved, I asked him, "*you* have to have things approved?" I couldn't believe that. But when you are working in a dimension that involves so much money and so many people, there are other people who have things to say, and you have to listen to them.

So if your freedom would be limited in film, what is the attraction for you?

The way to go would be to make independent films on a low budget so that you can do exactly as you please. That would be the way to go, but no one is giving me any money to do this—and why should they? I have no track record, really.

But you have worked on a lot of films, Michael.

Fourteen films. Its a twenty-hour-a-day job, but I have complete control (almost) in my work. That would have been a great way to go, and I might have been able to do OK working in films. I always felt I could do it. But on the other side of the coin, if you really want to do it, you do it *no matter what*. So did I really want to do it? I don't know.

When people write about you in the future, is there a genre you would like to be known for in terms of the work you did, in film, on Broadway, in the ballet world, or as artistic director or performer?

That's a good question. I don't know how to answer it, I really don't. I make dances. That's what I do. Most people don't start out life thinking, "One day I am going to direct a ballet company." But I did. From the time I was just a little punk, I knew that one day I would have my own ballet company, so I spent my life preparing myself for the time it would happen. I *loved* performing, but from the very beginning I wanted to choreograph.

You are an unusual artist in the sense that you have done so much in different areas of dance and have been successful in each of those realms.

Whatever it is, it's all choreography. It's funny how one thing can spur something else to happen. You can do a Pert hair commercial, and when you go back to choreographing a ballet to Bach, it does influence it. I am not sure how, but it does. It's about keeping your eyes open.

As a child, I had dyslexia, and I still do. I would start a sentence in the middle, read from the middle to the end and the middle to the beginning, and I didn't know that I did it that way. Remember when you were a kid and you had to stand up in class and read? I would read aloud and everyone would laugh and I wondered what they were laughing at.

Did you know that you were seeing differently from your classmates?

I knew what I was reading. When I was working on *Warriors,* I remember I went to Berkeley to be tested because I was mixing up phone numbers, and I thought that maybe there was some way of treating this. They gave me puzzles to put together and three-dimensional chess and all of this stuff. It was about ten days of testing. Afterwards, I was told that if I were a physicist or an accountant, I would have a big problem, but the fact that I make dances and choreograph means that what I was suffering from was a blessing. I see things no one else sees.

Can you tell me more about when you won the Fred Astaire Award? That was a terrific year for you.

That was a great award, for the choreography in *Anything Goes*. That year, I won a Tony. I am probably the only choreographer who has a Tony, an Emmy, and a Fred Astaire Award and is running a company. Jerome Robbins received an Academy Award but not the Fred Astaire Award. The only other choreographer I can think of who has won an Emmy is Paul Taylor.

Where do you keep your trophies?

They are on the mantel in the living room. It's a wonderful feeling to be top dog, even if it's only for fifteen minutes, and then it's business as usual. Can you tell me who won the Academy Award for best actor this year? People usually forget. I didn't expect to win that Tony.

Have you ever considered writing a book about your dance career?

No. I am not going to go down in history as one of those people in the top level of choreography mainly because I am in California and I am not back East. But this is where I do my work, and there is a certain amount of snobbery where my work is concerned.

What do you mean?

When I am working on Broadway, I am the "ballet guy." When I work in ballet, I am the "Broadway guy." You can't be on both sides of the fence; you either have to be on one side or the other. You know, the line between modern dance and ballet is very thin sometimes, and my feeling is that movement is movement. Dance is dance, and we should incorporate the best of everything.

Critics often refer to your work as having a theatrical dimension. You understand the theatre, obviously, from your early training and performing experiences. Some critics don't recognize this talent as a positive one. How do you see it?

I do. The word *theatre* used to be a verb. I rest my case. You don't want to sit there and say, "Now, what are they doing onstage and why are they doing it?" Then you have the intellectual critic telling you that this is what it all means. No kidding.

There is a lot of flack about Michael Flately and his show "Riverdance." People say that he is just a carnival man, but when you see 6,000 people stand up and scream "Bravo," why does that happen? Because he doesn't know what he is doing? Give the guy a break! He was able to take the art form that was practically unknown and bring it to the level of a rock concert. Those halls are filled. This guy is making a million dollars a week. I just love it for a dancer to make a million dollars a week. Just give this guy his just due. He is pretty damn terrific.

Do you read reviews?

I never read my own, but I read everyone else's.

Are their any critics whose writing you like especially?

I think there are some very good writers. I think that Arlene Croce is a very good writer, because when you read something that she wrote, you feel as if you have seen the performance. With some other writers, I wonder, "Where the hell were they?" What I mean is that I was at the theatre and I saw that performance, and that is not what happened.

There was a time when I was just starting training in the 50s and the critics were educators; they were gentleman of letters, and they would report what they saw in the theatre without being bitchy, without being vile, and without making a lot of people squirm.

It was about the art form, not the artist. Who did you admire? Who comes to mind?

Yes, it was about the art form. For example, Al Freed, Robert Commanday, Edwin Denby—they were gentleman and educators. Now it seems like so many people are writing gossip columns rather than writing about how the company did.

When you were having problems with the San Francisco Ballet, there were many mean-spirited articles written about you. How did that criticism affect you?

It was difficult. It boiled down to one person undermining me, to the point where I had to go. I had a board that was behind me, and obviously I had an audience. It's a thing of the past. Everybody at one time in their life, or most everybody, is fired from a job, and its just as traumatic to be fired from a gas station as it is when you are the director of a top ballet company. It takes time for that to heal.

Was that the worst time in your artistic life?

I suppose so, because when I came back to San Francisco, I thought that this is where I would finish, and when I walked out of San Francisco Ballet it would be in a pine box, so it was very strange. When I came to San Francisco Ballet, the company was performing in gymnasiums. I was able to put them on national television twelve times. We went to Europe; we danced at the White House. We built an audience, and then at the peak of our success, I am fired. It can't be because of my work. It has to be from a Machiavellian undermining of the situation, and of course that was what it was.

How did you cope?

I felt that I dealt with it up-front and honestly. If I had been just a little more sophisticated, I would have played hardball in the back rooms the way my opposition did. They were totally dishonest and very nasty.

But after you left San Francisco Ballet, new doors opened to you in your career.

There is certainly no question about that. It's a no-win situation directing a huge city company like that because you are damned if you do and you are damned if you don't. You can't be all things to all people. You just have to do the best you can and let the chips fly. It's different now with Smuin Ballets/SF, because I have my audience who come to see my work because they want to.

That must feel quite good for you.

It is very freeing. It's also terribly selfish, but it's a wonderful kind of selfishness since it's so wonderfully indulgent. But I think I didn't go far enough when I was at San Francisco Ballet. Some people thought I went too far.

Michael, when you had your heart attack, how did your life change?

The thing about my heart attack is I didn't experience it. Everybody else experienced it. I had no warning. All of a sudden it was lights out. Then for three days I would wake up and go to sleep, wake up and go to sleep, wake up and go to sleep. Finally, I woke up and said, "What happened?" I had no idea what it was all about.

You don't remember any of it?

No. I went to therapy and they said I would remember everything, and I didn't remember anything. It did change my outlook though. I had a cholesterol level that was 380, and I thought I was in perfect condition. Now its 130. I exercise vigorously every day, I take some medication, and I am basically a vegetarian except for eating chicken and fish.

Did the heart attack change you emotionally?

Maybe in a lot of ways I didn't realize. People find me very different. They tell me that I have mellowed.

I would like to speak about your company and how you choose the performers. When you have auditions, obviously you look for more than prowess and technical skills. What else do you look for?

You look for nice, hunky guys who look like men onstage and can lift and turn and jump and act. You demand a certain amount of beauty with the women; when that curtain goes up you want to have some beauty on the stage. After that, you look for determination. You look for people who will work hard, who have brains and musicality. But I think musicality is the number one thing I look for.

Do you think that musicality can be taught or is it innate?

I think a lot of it can be taught. The dancers who are really good just have it, whether they played an instrument or sang in the chorus or in church. It doesn't matter; they just have it. When I worked with really musical dancers like Celia [Fushille-Burke], Evelyn [Cisneros], or Cynthia [Gregory], they are really supreme musicians. They don't even know it, but they are. When you work with those people you find yourself frequently rethinking your choreography in terms of the music and in terms of how they phrase.

When you choreograph, do you think about what is pleasing for you or are you thinking about the audience and what they will respond to?

You think of all those things. You want things that the dancers do to work for an audience, but on the other hand, you don't want them to do anything physically that is going to hurt them. Sometimes I may get carried away and think that something is really great. But the dancer may be so sore the next day so the step or the lift is cut.

Do you like to create on their bodies?

I have to. I become that body. I crawl right into the skin of that body.

Would you change the choreography if a dancer has trouble with the phrasing?

Yes. I might change something dramatically, and I may even say after working with them, "Oh God, that should not be danced this way, that should be danced this way." Or, I may even say, "You know the way you did that? That was not what I wanted, but now it's what I want you to do, because you phrased the whole passage differently."

When I worked with Evelyn, it happened a lot during the making of *A Song for Dead Warriors* and *Tempest*. I found myself rephrasing things for her music, the music that was in her body. It happens often with women, but not too much with the guys.

How much of a dancer's body reflects the creation of the work?

Enormously. That's why a lot of times some of my ideas don't translate so well, because it doesn't go on the body that I did it on originally. Recasting the body is always a ticklish proposition. When I choreograph, I crawl inside a body to see what it can do. Two sopranos singing the same aria will sound different. It's the same for two dancers: When they perform the exact same steps, they will look different.

Do you notate your work?

I do, but no one can read it but me. It's not really notated. I think that between the notes in my score, the videotape, and the notes that I make and the dancers memories, we can usually reconstruct the work fairly accurately.

When you look at videotape, are you able to see the nuances in the work?

The problem with videotape is that you never get a perfect performance, so when people reconstruct from videotape, you also reconstruct mistakes. That happens all the time.

So you remember earlier pieces from years ago? Do you have a precise visual memory?

No, but I know when it's wrong. I know when it's off the music, but I don't remember absolutely the specific steps in sequence. My wife Paula does. She has a photographic memory. There are some people in my company who have complete photographic memories. I think I have some type of erase system, and the minute that I have something done, I am getting ready for the next thing.

That is probably healthy, creatively speaking, because you are fresh and you can get a clean perspective on the work.

But you have to get rid of a lot of information in order to make room for the information. I don't really know how it happens, but I know that I have always been that way.

How about your dreams, Michael? I remember you told me once that dreams help you. Do you write them down?

The problem with dreams is by the time I wake up, I usually have forgotten what they are. Sometimes I can force myself to wake up and will make notes, but sometimes I can't even read those notes in the morning. Sometimes I have a dream and it's a great idea and I get up and write it down, and it actually works.

Are you an active day dreamer?

Oh yeah. I get images all the time. Sometime, I am listening to a piece of music and I will see a specific dancer and maybe even part-nered by someone specific. I can see things happen.

In terms of actual choreography, do you actually see the move-ments in your mind's eye? Can you give me an example?

Yes. I made a dance for one of the dancers in *Carmina.* In the dance two guys bring her on stage on two poles and she is hanging on with her feet. A lot of the movements for this piece I saw in a day-dream. Some of it worked and some of it didn't.

What about computer programs? Have you ever used them, or does that interest you at all?

You know, I am afraid to start. I am afraid to start because I have a feeling that it may be so fascinating that I would create these won-derful things and would never get into the studio.

Do you think that you would feel lost in the process of making the work?

That's right. I think that I would be captivated by the possibilities of what you can do with the computer. I would be hooked—strapped to that chair and that computer. I would never get to the studio.

I have avoided it on purpose. Once I started, I would be stuck, be-cause the possibilities are endless. I would be so disappointed with making this masterpiece on the computer and then taking it to the studio and having nothing work.

When you stopped dancing, was it a conscious decision?

I never knew that I did. I came out to direct the San Francisco Ballet when I was thirty-three years old. I was so busy teaching and choreo-graphing and putting on performances and doing everything a director does that three years later, I realized that I hadn't been onstage.

Since it was more of an evolutionary transition, perhaps it was easier for you?

I think that all of the stuff I did before—Broadway, the nightclub circuit, television work—all of it was geared to directing and choreographing; that's what I always wanted to do. So it wasn't a wrenching and traumatic thing to quit dancing, unlike the experiences of some of my colleagues. I never danced to dance. I only danced so I could choreograph. Dancing was not the end-all for me. I always wanted to make dances, and that was true from the very beginning.

You mean, when you were a kid you knew?

Yes. I wasn't happy with the dance lessons I received as a kid from my teachers. I would go home and make up my own dances. I remember my mother took me to a performance of the Ballets Russes when I was about seven years old. I asked her, "How come they don't bump into each other? Who tells them where to go? Is it the same performance every night? How do they do that?" So the mechanism was there; the seeds of the work as a choreographer were there at the beginning.

What were you like as a child? Can you describe yourself?

I was the kind of kid who wanted to take the back off a watch to see how it worked because I wasn't happy to see what time it was. I wanted to know more. I wanted to know how the parts worked. I was making dances as a kid because I had to. I didn't even know what the word *choreographer* meant at that age, but that was what I was doing. I was making dance. I think that is the difference with a lot of choreographers. Choreographers choreograph because they must, just like writers write because they must.

Michael, you paint and sculpt. Are those activities relaxing for you, or are they just other artistic forms you *must* do?

I paint and draw all the time. I like to sculpt because it is fun to work with my hands, and no one talks back to you. I also read all the time. It's a terrific escape. Gardening is also another form of absolute escape for me.

What are you reading now?

Michael Smuin (right) and his wife, Paula Tracy-Smuin (center), with Ed Sullivan (left). *Photographer unknown. Reproduced by permission of Michael Smuin.*

I like Balanchine, Robbins, Ashton, Kylian. I think that Eliot Feld is the most underrated of our American choreographers. There is a real mind at work when he is choreographing a ballet. It may be repetitive and he may be in need of an editor sometimes, but his work is always intelligent. It's never frivolous, and if it is, that's his purpose.

Michael, what are your thoughts about the future of dance?

I thinks it's a hard time now, and it's certainly not like the ballet boom in the middle 1970s or 1980s. Now you can't use a full orchestra, or you have to use a small orchestra or none at all. We use CDs. There are companies that can't exist now because of the way the funding is, and the tax laws have changed. I want to continue making work and touring and performing with my company in the future.

Can you imagine doing anything else with your life?

I would probably be a rancher, because that is where I came from. I would be under the blue skies, and I would be running a big ranch someplace.